CAROLINA INDIANS

Dedicated to the memory of my son Daniel, who insisted that since this land belongs to the Indians, we should return it to them.

These stories, based upon both fact and legend, discuss the relationship between the Europeans and Carolina Indians.

Golden Age Press

Other Books By Author:

Cedar Island Past and Present Vol I
Cedar Island Past and Present Vol II
Wild Ponies of the Outer Banks
A Walk in the Night
Sea, Sand, and Settlers
Cedar Island Fisher Folks
Blackbeard Terror of the Seas
Banker Ponies

Copyright 1998 by Jean Day
Library of Congress # 98-92904
ISBN # 1-890 238-49-X

Art Editor: Douglas Campbell

Printed by Griffin & Tilghman
New Bern NC

Golden Age Press
Newport NC

Table of Contents:

INTRODUCTION:

We call them Indians. But this is a misnomer.

In 1492 when Christopher Columbus sailed from Spain, he was under the mistaken belief that Asia lay across from the Atlantic Ocean. At that time the "civilized world" was not aware that when traveling west, North and South America separated Europe from Asia.

When he found land, Columbus was confused and called the natives, "Indians." Even after he had been proven wrong, the name still clung.

Now those we call "Indians" prefer the term, "Native Americans." This is better. But just as all other Americans originally came from other places, so did the "Native Americans."

Man didn't originate in the Americas. In fact archaeological and geological experts say the early Americans were Mongoloids, who 10,000 to 28,000 years ago, crossed from northeastern Siberia on a land bridge at the Bering Straits to Alaska.

Huge herds of mammoths, camels, horses, and bison trampled trails in the snow as they crossed back and forth over the bridge. Since the Early Hunters depended on the animals for food, they followed the trails made by the herds. Gradually they multiplied and spread over what is now North and South America. They had bows and arrows, used primitive spears, and didn't know how to farm or make pottery. Food was roasted over fires built around piles of stones or by being dropped in a skin-lined pit with hot rocks on the bottom. They lived and traveled in small family groups, wherever the herds of game led them, depending entirely upon the animals for food except for a few nuts and berries gathered by the women.

For several thousand years the Early Hunters lived the same way, some in the Piedmont and eastern regions of North Carolina.

After the mammoths became extinct, the Indians gathered food as well as hunted, and were called Hunters and Gatherers. Since they liked clams, shell mounds mark the same places they returned to each year to trade, feast, and socialize. A few tribes remained and established villages near the shell mounds. The women gathered roots and bark to grind into edible food. The spears the men hunted with were greatly improved by this time. Evidence of this culture has been found throughout the Carolinas.

As the Indians settled down, they depended more upon the corn and beans and other vegetables they raised. They were called Early Farmers. Since each tribe made their own individual form of pottery, the shards of clay pots found in various locations identifies the tribes which lived there. Some of their ceremonial pipes were finely crafted of polished stone and handed down from generation to generation. Because the Early Farmers remained in the same location, they built more substantial houses.

The Indians lived in this manner until the white man came and gave them white man's diseases, killed some outright, and took many away as slaves.

The Carolina Indians differed in several ways from the Plains Indians out West. Although horses were here as early as 1500 AD, the Carolina Indians didn't ride them until the white man arrived. They could run in the woods faster than the white men could ride their horses.

Instead of living in teepees, the Carolina Indians built houses, some rather large, framed with logs, and covered with bark or woven reeds.

The Carolina Indians agreed with the Plains Indians as to the beginning of mankind and the hereafter. They also agreed that man cannot own land. It is here to be used and left in the same condition it was found. Unless disturbed, they were more peaceful than their Plains brothers.

When the white men came, they discovered a thriving, self-sufficient people with an advanced culture and religion. They immediately set about to reform the natives to fit their own ideas of what was proper.

The following stories have been collected from many different, often conflicting sources.

PRINCE MADOC MEETS THE INDIANS

Most folks believe that the first Europeans the Carolina Indians met were either Spanish or French. But this wasn't necessarily so. Legend tells us they could have been Welsh.

In 1138, in the Welsh province of Gwyneth, Prince Owen succeeded his father as ruler. He ruled for 38 years, years marred by bloody warfare between the Norman barons and Welsh chieftains. His attempt to unite the various Welsh kingdoms into one country caused the English to refer to him as the "King of Wales."

In 1169, King Owen Gwyneth died without naming which of his 17 sons should succeed him as ruler. The questionable legitimacy of his sons muddied the issue. Civil war broke out over who would be king.

But Owen's youngest son Madoc, who was a seafaring man, wanted no part of either the war or of the throne. The story of Madoc has been repeated generation after generation despite concentrated efforts to refute the validity of the tale. Since land held no allure for him, Madoc gathered some of his followers and made plans to leave his war-torn island in search of a new land where he and his followers hoped to be able to live in peaceful harmony.

They sailed west across the Atlantic Ocean without knowing exactly where they were going. But Madoc was certain there would be land at the end of the ocean.

He was correct.

They landed on the coast of what would later be Virginia. They were met by bronze-skinned natives, who were under the impression that these strange white, bearded creatures were gods. Here the settlers found an ocean teeming with fish, woods filled with deer and bear, and soil rich enough to grow crops.

Although the settlers were in many ways self-sufficient, there were certain things which could only be obtained in Europe. And then too, some of the settlers had family and friends they wanted to have join them in this new land.

Soon after the colonists had settled in, Prince Madoc selected certain of his men to accompany him back to Wales for needed supplies and additional settlers.

Anxious months, then years passed with no word from Prince Madoc. Gradually the colonists learned to live like Indians, and the two groups mingled to become one tribe, some with light skins and red hair. Apparently they retained a form of their Welsh language.

But this was far from the end of the Prince Madoc story.

When he returned to Wales, Prince Madoc fitted out ten more ships and filled them with supplies, settlers, and munitions for his second trip to the new land. His plan was to return to his colony in Virginia. However, ocean currents carried them further south into the Gulf of Mexico and Mobile Bay.

From here, he and his followers traveled up the Alabama River into Tennessee and western North Carolina. As they moved onward, they left crumbling mounds and fortifications at Lookout Mountain and from the Little Tennessee River on into Kentucky. Archaeologists say these forts are pre-Columbian in structure and far beyond the engineering capabilities of the Indians, and that the fort on top of Lookout Mountain bears a striking resemblance to one at Madoc's home in Wales.

Some of the Welsh settled in the beautiful spacious mountains and valleys of the great Smokies. The Old Men of the Cherokee Nation tell stories of people with red hair, white skins, and bearded faces, with eyes the blue of the sky, who lived in their beloved mountains before the Spaniards came seeking gold. These strange men lived in houses dug out of the mountain, and constructed of logs and mud.

Once during the full moon--no one knows when-- fierce Creeks came up from the South and chased the Welsh Settlers into Tennessee, then on out West. Here they became the Mandan tribe. They lived in houses built like those of the Cherokee-Welsh Indians. They made Welsh-type round, hide-covered, light-weight wicker boats which could easily be lifted from the sea and filled with water to bathe in.

One of the first writers to verify the story of Madoc was renowned geographer-historian Richard Hakluyt. His writings are generally accepted by British and American authorities. The sources he refers to in his work, "Principall Navigations (1600), establishes that the story of Madoc existed before Columbus' time. This disproves the theory that the British put forth the Madoc story in order to establish Great Britains's rights to the New World.

Governor John Seiver of Tennessee wrote of a time he spent with the Cherokee in 1782 when he had a conversation with Cherokee Chief Oconosta. The chief said his grandfather told him, "The people who built the fortifications were Welsh, who had crossed the great Water and landed at Mobile Bay."

In 1738 French explorer Sieur de la Verendrye visited the Mandan villages and kept a detailed journal. At this time the people numbered 15,000 in eight villages. His report reads much like Lewis' and Clark's letters to President Jefferson in 1804 when they spent a winter in a Mandan village. They described the "Indians" as white men and women whose towns were laid out in squares with a statue much like a cross in the center. "The men had beards and grey hair, and the women were beautiful," they wrote.

George Catlin, who painted many Indian portraits, visited the Mandans in 1841. At this time, the numbers had decreased by two-thirds. He speculated that these people were descended from Madoc's lost colony. His work includes several pages of vocabulary comparing the Mandan language with the Welsh. He was surprised to find the Mandans with various shades of skin and hair. He said, "They had blue or grey eyes and European facial features, and when they grow old, their hair turns white, unlike other Indian tribes."

Catlin added, "The women are beautiful and sexual and babble while being embraced much as the Welsh girls do."

In spite of those who refuse to believe these stories, the Daughters of the American Revolution erected a bronze tablet at Mobile Bay, inscribed, "In memory of Prince Madoc, a Welsh explorer, who landed on the shores of Mobile Bay in 1170, and left behind with the Indians, the Welsh language."

However, these people who had survived the trip across the Atlantic Ocean, because their blood was mixed with the Indians, lost their natural immunity to the white man's diseases. Many died in a small pox epidemic. Because of this, the Mandan tribe is now considered extinct.

Back in Eastern North Carolina, the remnants of Madoc's first expedition apparently survived.

In 1669, Morgan Jones, a Welsh preacher, sailed south from Virginia to bring the Gospel to the Indians. However, because of the many hardships he endured off the coast of North Carolina, he decided to return to Virginia.

But along the banks of the Pamlico River, he was captured by a group of Doeg Indians, a branch of the Tuscarora tribe. He noted that many of them had fair skins and red hair. He was confined under guard in a small hut while the council met to determine his fate.

Jones stood in the doorway and anxiously observed the meeting. One eloquent warrior waved his arms and pointed his finger accusingly at him.

Suddenly young warriors surrounded Jones and bound his hands and feet. When the Indians began a frenzied, uncontrolled dance, he knew his fate--he was to die. He pulled himself to his knees as best he could and prayed over and over again in his Welsh tongue, "Oh, God, have I escaped so many dangers that I must now be knocked on the head like a dog? Lord, preserve me and keep me from all harm. Grant me the courage to face tomorrow."

He noticed one man who stood apart from the others and watched and listened to his prayers, almost as if he understood the meaning of his words.

When morning came, this same man, who proved to be the chief, came to Jones and cut his bonds. "You will not be killed," he said. "You speak with my tongue. How can this be?"

Jones didn't understand it either, but when he heard the chief speak, he realized that what he heard, was a garbled version of his own language.

So Jones remained for a time to preach among the Doegs. Many later agreed with him that these Indians were descended from Prince Madoc's first settlement.

Those who have traveled among the various Indian tribes of both the East and the West, say they have been unable to locate any Welsh-speaking Indians. However, this does not prove they did not exist.

NATIVES MEET THE SPANISH

When Columbus discovered the natives he called Indians, he considered them inferior, fit only to be servants. In the beginning he tried to buy their friendship by presenting them with glass beads and other cheap trinkets, but then his true nature revealed itself.

He massacred some, but still not satisfied, he tricked 1100 of them to come aboard his four ships, intending to sell them as slaves. However his plan was doomed to failure. The ships were so overloaded, it caused sickness. On the trip to Spain, they ran into a storm where many were washed overboard. Only 300 survived.

Thus Columbus set the precedent for the leaders of the Spanish expeditions which followed. They came seeking riches. Their plan was to conquer and then evangelize the natives, by force if necessary.

When the heads of the European nations learned about this new land, naturally they wanted their share of the wealth and power it represented. The fact that other people lived there, had for many generations, didn't faze them in the least. They considered it theirs for the taking.

Spain, France, and England didn't gather around a conference table to decide who should have what. Spain didn't say, "I want it all, but I'll settle for the southern part."

And England didn't say, "Give me the mid-Atlantic coast."

And France didn't say," I don't like it, but that leaves me the land beyond the mountains."

Instead of this, claiming and settling the land was slow, fraught with danger, disappointment, and death.

GORDILLO

In 1520 Luces Vasquez de Ayllon, a Spanish official, slave trader, and explorer sent sea captain Francisco Gordillo to the New World to explore this mysterious land rumored to be inhabited by giants.

The two ships had an uneventful crossing until they arrived within sight of land. A violent storm drove them into the mouth of a river they called Jordan. As the ships slowly advanced up river, curious crewmen searched the shore for any sign of life.

"Over there--two men."

Gordillo ordered his mate, "Take a landing party in small boats to investigate."

The natives were curious about these strange vessels and the men who manned them. A tall one who was naked except for a breech clot said, "Such disgusting-looking creatures--like animals with hair hiding their faces."

Another one, who was younger, agreed, "No Indian would allow hair to grow on his face like that. They must be animals of a type we don't know." They fled in terror but were soon captured and taken before Gordillo.

"What'll we do with them?" the mate asked.

"Dress them in Spanish clothes and send them back."

So it was done. When the Indians returned to their people dressed as Spaniards, the chief asked, "Did they harm you?"

"No, I think they want to be friends. Reassured by this, the tribal chief sent a delegation of Indians to meet the Spaniards.

Gordillo went ashore with some of his men. There he claimed the land in the name of King Charles V of Spain by carving crosses on several large trees. The men remained three weeks to trade with the Indians for furs and pearls.

When Gordillo invited some unsuspecting Indians aboard his ship, unable to believe he meant them any harm, they followed him. The tour ended in the holds of the ships.

"Raise sails!" Gordillo ordered. The ships slipped away from shore with the Indians captive aboard. They sailed for Hispaniola with approximately 150 Indians as slaves. On the way, one ship was lost. The surviving captives and crew were crowded on the remaining ship. Eventually they arrived safely at Hispaniola.

Since the Indians were especially large in stature, Gordillo thought they would make good slaves. But instead he found them to be not malleable, homesick, and lazy. Since some refused to eat the strange food set before them, they starved to death.

One of the prisoners who survived was called Francisco Chicora by the Spaniards. After he learned to speak Spanish, he related amazing stories about his home land. "Deep in the mountains lives a race of men who have long, flexible tails."

The Spanish roared with laughter at the foolish antics of this crazy Indian.

But Chicora went on,

"These people have to cut holes in their chairs to accommodate their tails."

He spoke with such sincerity that some began to wonder if what he said was true. "The priests use a magic balm to stretch the bones of royal children. And the land is fertile beyond measure."

The Spaniards thought him amusing, but when he said, "The gold is as stones holding up the mountains," he had all their attention.

DE AYLLON

De Ayllon decided this was something he had to see for himself. So he organized another expedition with six ships to find this wondrous land he called "Chicora" in honor of the Indian slave.

His group had over 500 men and women with slaves and 80 to 90 horses. All went well until they entered the mouth of the Cape Fear River, where one of their ships carrying supplies, struck a shoal and tore open the hull. The smaller ships took on the survivors and anchored off shore. Most of their foodstuffs were lost.

"Is this the correct place?" de Ayllon asked Chicora.

A huge grin spread across the Indian's face. "Yes, yes, this is the place," Chicora agreed. So he and several other Indians were put ashore to announce their arrival. Before he disappeared into the woods, Chicora turned around and laughed in glee at the stupidity of the Spaniards, eager to return to his tribe and tell them about these ignorant white skinned people who lived beyond the great ocean.

De Ayllon had been duped. He was furious and shook his fist at the disappearing Indians. "Where is the gold and silver and long-tailed natives?" he muttered to himself. "Chicora told those weird tales just to get a ride home." His men smothered their amusement behind grimy hands.

The Spanish lingered at Cape Fear long enough for the seamen to construct a small single masted ship which would utilize both oars and sails to replace the wrecked one. After wandering about, searching for a suitable site for their colony, many were sick.

The supplies they had brought with them were almost gone with no way to replenish them in this hostile land.

The location de Ayllon eventually chose for his settlement was in a low marshy area. He ordered the slaves to begin building houses for the settlers.

They called their settlement San Miguel. The lack of sufficient food caused the people to become weakened, susceptible to disease. They had expected the natives to aid them. But since this was the same people Gordillo had visited and taken many away as slaves, they refused to help. They had hoped to discover gold and silver. They found none. This caused great unrest among the people. Instead of riches, malaria quickly spread among the starving group, killing 200. On October 18, 1526, de Ayllon himself died of the deadly disease.

After de Ayllon's death, the settlement was taken over by Francisco Gomez. Because they had received nothing but hunger and poverty instead of the wealth they had been promised, many of the settlers rebelled.

As if this wasn't bad enough, some of the slaves, encouraged by the Indians, took this opportunity to set fires. They escaped to the woods. Here the native Americans took them in as sisters and brothers. The blacks' knowledge of farming and of the white way of life contributed to form a solid colony of black Indians.

By the time Gomez regained power, the conditions at San Miguel were hopeless. Only 150 of the original 500 remained. The Indians were hostile. No crops had been planted and another winter was approaching. The surviving Spanish left their crude log homes and boarded their ships to return to Hispaniola.

Here their bad luck continued, a storm came, seven passengers froze to death, and the ship which was carrying de Ayllon's body sank.

HERNANDO DE SOTO

In March of 1540, De Soto and his army left their winter quarters in Florida and began the long march which ended at the Mississippi. When he arrived at a town, the Indians usually welcomed him. He demanded their stored food, pearls, carriers, and women. Then he captured the chief to guide him on to the next town.

In May he reached the province of Cofitachequi in South Carolina. He had heard of a rich princess, Chualiah, who ruled that land. When the great chief died, since he had no sons, he had made his daughter ruler of a large tribe.

The Princess too had heard of De Soto and wanted to meet this powerful stranger. She made preparations for a feast and crossed the river to graciously welcome the explorers.

She was richly dressed in furs and feathers and decorated with precious gems. De Soto found Chualiah attractive and presented her with a large ruby ring. He decided he wanted her for himself. So he took her with him as his wife. Chauliah promised to lead him to the gold. But instead she led him on a long complicated journey.

Then a sudden barrage of deadly arrows flew through the air. Men fell off their beasts. As quickly as battle had begun, it was over.

When De Soto returned to camp, he noticed that Chauliah was missing.

Where is my woman?" he roared.

No one knew. Then he discovered that Franko, an Indian slave, was also missing. "Did they steal anything?" one of his captains asked.

De Soto went immediately to the place where he had

hidden a cache of pearls taken from the Indian princess. "It is gone." He was furious. "That thieving bitch! She stole my pearls. When I find her, I'll carve her heart out."

Of course he never found her.

De Soto with his men hiked on westward beyond the Mississippi. He died in the spring of 1542 near the site of what is now Memphis, never having found the gold.

The rumors of gold brought other Spanish expeditionary forces to Carolina. One man followed the lure of gold even after being shot in the mouth by an Indian arrow.

MENENDEZ

During the early part of 1566, Spain sent a man named Menendez with a small fleet north from St. Augustine, Florida along the Georgia and Carolina coasts. He mentioned meeting tribes in towns of Guale and Orista and entered the same harbor the French had earlier deserted.

On Paris Island, he built a fort he called Santa Elena. He made it the capital of his huge holdings.

Then in July a troop of 250 men arrived from Spain with Capt. Juan Pardo. They set to and began building a better fort and more substantial houses.

Menendez looked about and was pleased with what he saw. He met with his leaders and suggested, "I wonder if it is possible to go from here through the wilderness to New Spain [Mexico]. Since there are rich mines in Mexico, perhaps there are other rich mines along the way."

The word "gold" set their minds afire--they wanted their share of riches. It was decided to send a party of 120 soldiers under Juan Pardo to find out. A young Frenchman that the Indians had rescued when left behind joined them as guide.

Pardo wrote of the Indian settlements he visited, including a large settlement named Cofitachequi.

He went on to the town of Jora at the foothills of the Appalachians where he built a fort. Here he left behind a company of men under Sgt. Hernando Moyano de Morales. Then Pardo turned east again where he met with 30 Indian chiefs. He received a note from Santa Elena concerning the French which caused him to return to Santa Elena.

But before he left, he stationed four soldiers and his chaplain at Gustari, establishing the first successful Christian mission in what is now the United States.

In the spring of 1567, Sgt. Moyano sent a letter from the fort at the foothills of the Mountains, stating that he was having problems with the Indians. It began immediately after Pardo left him. Somehow Moyano insulted the chief of a Chisca tribe who lived on the far side of the mountains. Several messages passed back and forth. The chief sent the message, "Tell Moyano that I will eat him and his dog as well."

Now this was enough to strike fear into the heart of a brave man. Perhaps this is the origin of the rumor that a group of cannibal Indians lived in the western part of South Carolina.

Moyano wasn't going to sit there and allow those savages to come take him, so he went on the offensive. He crossed over the mountains to the fortified village where the angry Chisca chief lived. Moyano and his men stormed the entrance. Even though Moyano was wounded in the fray, he and his men forced the fort. The families who were not located within the fort, were killed in the woods.

Moyano set fire to the fort and houses. The smell of smoke and death filled the air. Black smoke and red flames rose high in the sky, a gigantic funeral pyre. More than 1,000 Indians were said to have died there that day.

This was only one of the Chisca tribes. After the fire, Moyano took his men down the valley of the Nolichucky River to the main body of the Chisca..

Having already heard about Moyano's victory over the first chief, 3,000 warriors met him in peace. Moyano built a fort and settled down to await further orders.

Meanwhile Menendez listened to Pardo's account of his trip. He decided to send Pardo out again. He followed De Soto's route on a trail leading up the Wateree to the town of Cofitachequi on the river bank outside the present Camden, South Carolina.

He went on to what is now Charlotte, North Carolina, then he met Moyano at Chisca.

Jesuit missionaries arrived to bring the faith to the Indians. One priest complained, "They make sport of what I say. They keep asking such foolish questions as, "Does God have a wife?"

The Jesuits withdrew.

Eventually Spain gave up her rights to the Carolinas.

NATIVES MEET THE FRENCH

VERRAZANO

The first European credited to having explored the North Carolina coast was Giovonni da Verrazano, an Italian navigator, sailing under the auspices of France.

In 1524 he sailed along the coast of Cape Fear, then traveled north along the Outer Banks. Great fires could be seen burning along the shore.

"One thing is certain, this place is inhabited." This didn't worry Verrazano. Although he had never been this far north before, he had no reason to believe the inhabitants would be anything but peaceful.

"What are we going to do about fetching water? We're running low." The ship's quartermaster cast a worried glance at the rough seas.

"Take 25 men with you and go ashore with gifts of paper, glasses, bells, and such-like for the natives and fetch some water."

The sea was rough. As the boat was lowered overboard, it almost capsized in the billowing waves. The men's muscles bulged as they attempted to row ashore, but the constant beating of the waves against the boat made progress slow. "It is hopeless. There is no way we can land or even get close enough to wade ashore," the quartermaster said.

Crowds of bronze-skinned people gathered on the

beach. They appeared to be friendly. This was probably the first white men they had seen, yet they exhibited no fear. "The only way we'll ever reach shore is to swim. Who'll volunteer?" Although most of the men had spent their lives on or near the water, they couldn't swim.

No one spoke. Then the men pointed to Tom, the youngest man on board. Tom was barely more than a child with just a whisper of fuzz on his cheeks, but he could swim.

"Give this to the natives." The quartermaster handed Tom a package wrapped in an oilskin pouch. Tom removed his shoes and coat and plunged into the rough sea. He made good headway until he was about three or four yards from shore. The sight of so many strange, red faces frightened him. He heaved the bundle of gifts as far as he could. It landed on the sand. He became frantic and sank. He came up sputtering and began to tread water. He attempted to return to the boat. The furious waves beat him towards the one place he didn't want to go--the shore.

He floated on his back, exhausted, almost dead. A great wave broke towards him and threatened to carry him back out to sea, but he couldn't fight any more. He couldn't breathe. This was the end. He watched helplessly as Indians rushed towards him. With the sea on one side and the Indians on the other, he knew he was going to die.

When the boy felt their hands upon him he shook with fright and cried out, "Oh, my God, help me, I don't want to die!"

The Indians cried right along with him as they carried him ashore. They laid him on the ground at the foot of a sand dune. After they had removed his wet clothing, they ran their hands over his white skin, marveling at its lack of color.

They left him lying in the shelter of a sand dune while they built a huge fire nearby.

When the boy saw the fire, he trembled. They were going to roast him alive, then eat him. He had heard stories of the cruelty of the Indians, and now he believed them. He shook as if suffering from a great chill.

The men in the boat watched what was happening to the young boy. "They've got Tom, but what can we do?"

The quartermaster shook his head. "There's nothing we can do. Even if we could reach shore, they are so many and we are so few. It is better to lose one man than all of us. We must pray for Tom, that if they are to kill him, it will be sudden."

The Indians kept murmuring kind words of reassurance to Tom until gradually he stopped shivering and recovered his strength. He had begun to realize that the savages meant him no harm, but he wouldn't feel safe until he was back on the boat. He gestured, showing them he wanted to return to his friends.

The Indians clapped him on the shoulders to demonstrate their great love, embraced him, then followed him to the water's edge. They watched to make sure he reached the boat safely.

Back on the boat, his shipmates gathered around him and draped a wool blanket across his shoulders. "What were the people like?" the quartermaster asked.

"Their flesh is shiny, almost black. They are handsome. They cared for me like I was a little child. I was frightened at first, but they were friendly."

The quartermaster and his men returned to the ship and continued further up the coast until they came to a place where the boat was able to get closer to shore. Some of the men waded through the water to reach land.

The place appeared to be deserted. "The natives must have fled into the woods. I saw them when we were in the boat," one man said.

But all they could find was an old woman and a young maid of 18 or 20 years. The older woman carried two infants on her shoulders, and behind her neck a child of about eight. The young woman also carried several children. When they saw that escape was impossible, they hid in the tall grass.

As the men caught up with them, the old woman cried out, motioning that their men had gone off into the woods.

"Hey, let's feed them, then maybe we can talk with them," Tom suggested.

The old woman gobbled down the food, then thanked them profusely. But the young woman clamped her jaw tight with disdain, refusing their food.

One of the men took a small child from the old woman. She relinquished him with great reluctance. "Let's take him back to France with us." The seaman held him under his arm. When the old woman saw their intention, she began to cry.

Then another man suggested, "Hey, you take the child, I want the young woman."

One seaman grabbed her, another helped as they attempted to carry her back to the boat. But she screamed and wailed and fought. "Damn woman. It's like trying to carry a wild tiger." It was quite a distance through the woods to the shore where the boat was anchored.

"Damn vixen! She scratched my eyes." The seaman dropped her. She raced off to the woods. The men left, taking only the small child with them.

The men spent the next three days on the Outer Banks, filled their water casks, fished, clammed, and explored the land. Gradually the natives came closer but they made little contact with Verrazano's party. "Their skins are lighter than those we saw before," Tom said.

"It appears to me they must sleep out in the field," Verrazano observed. Later they saw dwellings far off in the woods, but they couldn't get close enough to get a good look. It appeared the houses were framed from wood and covered with bark. Leaves sewn together with threads of wild hemp modestly covered their private parts. Their heads were trussed. They lived by fishing and hunting.

Verrazano and his ship sailed on up the coast, leaving the Outer Banks behind. He sent an exaggerated description of the North Carolina coast to King Francis I in France.

Later on a trip to South America, Verrazano was captured, killed, and eaten by savages.

RIBAULT

On May 1, 1562, a French ship commanded by Protestant sea captain Jean Ribault, arrived off the coast of Florida. At this time, France and England were engaged in a religious war. Ribault followed the path of Ayllon to a place called Santa Elena. Here he built a wooden fortification for 30 men and named it Charlesfort.

Modern historians believe this site is buried under the concrete and railroad tracks of a shrimp dock close to State Highway 281 across Battery Creek near Port Royal, South Carolina.

Ribault carved crosses on trees and planted a stone column to claim the land for France.

Indians watched these strange white men as they built a fort, then the one who was obviously the leader, abandoned them to return home.

In France Ribault found his country under siege by a Catholic army, so he fled to England. Here he requested and received an audience with Queen Elizabeth. "And what is it I can do for you?" the Queen asked, her voice querulous.

She listened to his story. "Very well, I will assist you." But later when her advisors pointed out the wealth and power available in this New Land, she ordered, "Throw him in the tower."

"But you agreed to help him," one aide reminded her.

"I am Queen. I changed my mind."

Meanwhile Ribault's small garrison of men were stranded, surrounded by wilderness and Indians. The Indians didn't interfere. They didn't attack, but the men were afraid to go far from their fort. The commander, de Laudonniere, became irrational. He personally hanged one man and stranded another on a small island to starve.

The men mutinied and killed de Laudonniere. After rescuing their mate from the small island, they built a pitiful boat from pine, vines, and moss.

Then everyone boarded the boat except one 17 year-old boy. "No way will I trust my life to that pitiful excuse of a boat. It'll never make it out to sea, let alone home. I'd rather take my chances with the Indians," he said.

Surprisingly enough, the boat sailed safely away into the open Atlantic. But after 21 days, the winds died down and the boat was becalmed. The men were starving with no way to obtain either food or water. They were so hungry they ate their clothing, and overcome by thirst, they drank their own urine.

The situation was so desperate, one man whispered to another, "There is food here. It would be better if one man lose his life than all should die."

"But how do we decide who should die that the rest should live?" asked another.

They went to Capt. Barre, who was in charge, and put their plan to him. "No, we all live or we all die. What you are suggesting is murder."

But when he saw the homicidal terror in their eyes and the way they were watching him, he feared for his own life. "All right, you win." Knowing he might be signing his own death sentence, he said, "We draw lots."

The men held their breath as each man slowly revealed his straw. The one who drew the fatal lot was Lachere, who had been condemned to die on the small island by Ribault. His comrades pounced upon him, killed him, and divided his flesh among themselves.

By the time the boat drifted near the coast of Europe, the men were too weak to man the sails. An English patrol vessel picked them up. Since Nicolas Barre was French, he was clapped into the Tower of London. Perhaps he met his former captain, Ribault there.

Meanwhile Philip of Spain decided to move against Charlesfort. "That land belongs to me. No Frenchie can take it away from me." And he sent another expedition. When it arrived at Charlesfort, they discovered it abandoned. But the Indians brought the young man from Ribault's party, who had chosen to remain with the Indians instead of trusting his life to their makeshift boat.

Taking the young man with them, the Spanish moved further south where they built a new fortification located at San Mateo, Florida. They called it Fort Carolina.

Other Frenchmen came. They built a permanent settlement at Quebec and explored the great lakes and the immense wilderness in the heart of the continent.

By the early 1700s, the French controlled the two major gateways into the heart of North America, their fortified settlements at New Orleans and at Quebec.

France's interest in the New World was in trading and building a great sea power. They met the Indians on a more equal basis than the Spanish or English, often marrying and living among them.

NATIVES MEET THE ENGLISH

EXPLORATORY EXPEDITION

In the summer of 1584, Sir Walter Raleigh under the direction of Queen Elizabeth, sent an expedition to the New World for the purpose of exploring the possibility of establishing a settlement in what is now North Carolina.

Raleigh was the 30 year-old son of poor but distinguished parents. He had good schooling, experience in the French civil wars, and had commanded a ship in the fleet of Sir Humphrey Gilbert--his older half-brother.

He became a court favorite of Queen Elizabeth. She gave him control of the wine and wool industries. When Sir Gilbert died at sea, Raleigh asked to speak to the queen.

"I wish permission to colonize in North America. If we could establish a settlement there, it would be useful as a home port for privateers."

Because of the problems with Spain, England had issued licenses for legalized privateering. Queen Elizabeth listened to her paramour, and decided he made sense.

"Then too, your Majesty, Spain has become wealthy because of its colonization in the New World. Perhaps gold and other precious metals also exist in North America."

The Queen gave some thought to the matter, then prepared a paper granting Raleigh the right to establish a colony in the New World.

When his preparations were complete, Raleigh once again appeared before the Queen. "We will leave in two weeks," he said.

"Not you. I need you here at my side." Raleigh was disappointed, but no way could he disobey his queen. He chose Amandas and Barlowe as captains in his place. The force on the first expedition would be small, merely exploratory.

After a calm crossing, they reached land and followed the coast until they arrived at the Outer Banks of North Carolina. On the third day after the Englishmen's arrival, three natives appeared in a small boat beached at a safe distance down shore from the English vessels, One man left his companions and walked along the shore until he was opposite the English ship.

"They don't appear to be war-like," Barlowe said.

Barlowe and the navigator Ferdinando took Barlowe in a small boat to the land near where the native stood. He showed no fear, only curiosity. The white men were as curious about the red men as the red men were about them. The Indian proceeded to welcome them with a ponderous speech. The English didn't understand a word he said, but they understood he meant to be friendly.

By gestures they invited the Indian aboard their ship. Bravely he followed them. There they presented him with a shirt and hat and other gifts, then offered him wine and meat which he liked. He was taken on a tour of the other boat, then rowed back to shore. The English watched as he walked down the beach where a small boat was hidden.

"He seems friendly enough," Barlowe said. "I hope the natives are all as tame."

"He's dividing his fish into two piles. I wonder what

that's all about," Barlowe said.

The Indian gestured from a pile of fish to the pinnace, then from the other pile to the larger bark. "He means for us to have the fish," Ferdinando said. Then the Indian disappeared from sight.

He reported to his village what he had seen--the men with skins white as the belly of a whale, the ship many times the size of their longest canoe.

Anxious to witness this strange sight, the next morning more Indians appeared at the landing where the ships were anchored. They were led by Granganimeo, brother to the local weroance [king].

Barlowe and Amandas watched as the Indians walked along the shore until they were opposite the anchored ships. They spread a large woven mat on the sand for Granganimeo and four lesser warriors to sit on. More Indians stood in the background within sight of their leader, Granganimeo.

The English leaders launched a small boat and rowed to shore, holding their weapons in plain sight. They walked towards the Indians where Granganimeo and the other four leaders remained seated, showing no sign of fear.

The king beckoned for them to draw closer and sit beside him,. He made a long speech making signs of joy and welcome, striking on his head, and his breast, then on theirs to show they were brothers.

This first meeting led to extensive trade with the Indians. When Barlowe distributed gifts to the other chiefs, they whispered to each other, then deposited them on Granganimeo's lap. All gifts were to go through him, the others were only minions.

This was the Englishmen's introduction to the social order of the natives. "The king is greatly to be obeyed," Barlowe wrote, "and his brothers, and children reverenced." He also said that no people in the world had more respect for their king or chief than they did.

Barlowe and Amandas remained there for a few days, trading with the natives. The English traded a variety of merchandise including copper kettles, but most of this was of little value. In exchange the Indians offered furs.

One Indians had his eye on a tin plate. He fingered it longingly. He offered one deer skin,. Barlowe, seeing how much he wanted it, said, "No, no, much more."

The Indian offered two deer skins. Barlowe refused. Finally he accepted five deer skins for the tin plate.

"What do you want the plate for?" Barlowe asked.

He watched as the Indian punched a hole in the brim of it and hung it around his neck on a string. He made signs that it was to protect him from enemies' arrows.

Two days later, Granganimeo boarded the English ships, where he accepted wine. The next time he appeared, he was accompanied by his wife and an older daughter and two or three smaller children.

Indians came from miles around to see these strange people with the pale skins and to trade with them. Each day Granganimeo sent fresh meat. The Indians would have given all they possessed to trade for their hatchets, axes, knives, and swords, but the white men refused to part with them.

When one of his men wanted to accept a trade for his hatchet, Barlowe said, "No, don't you understand that it is these items which gives us superiority over them? If we share tools which could be used as weapons, they will use them against us."

The Indians let them know they were not to trade with other Indians, just those who "wear red pieces of copper on their heads. The other Indians are just common folks, not nobility like ourselves."

Finally Barlowe felt confident enough of the savages' good will to risk visiting them. He took a small boat with seven other men and headed for Granganimeo's village at the north end of the island. Most historians believe this is the modern day Roanoke, but because of the description in Barlowe's records, some historians are convinced Granganimeo's village was on what is now Cedar Island.

Before they even reached the village site, Granganimeo's wife ran out to greet them. She was short and dumpy with a grin as wide as her belly. Her husband was absent, but she ordered some of the Indian men to carry their guests on their backs to dry ground. "And bring their oars too, so no one will steal them," she said. The village contained nine houses, built of cedar, and fortified round about with sharp trees to keep out their enemies.

Granganimeo's wife led them into the main room of the largest house. "Sit down. Sit down by the fire." While she went to see about food preparation, her attendants attempted to remove the white men's clothes.

Barlowe allowed an Indian woman to remove his boots and told his companions, "Go along with it. We don't want to insult them." Their clothes were taken away to be washed and dried.

While they rested some of the women washed the men's feet in warm water. When their clothes were dry and the men were once again decently dressed, they were led to an interior room where a huge feast of roasted venison and fish, melons, fruit, and various boiled roots was set before them.

Barlowe looked up, nodded, and cautiously reached for his gun. "Men armed with bows and arrows are approaching.

Their hostess' quick black eyes detected his movement. "No, no. You are our guests." She pointed to the nearest servant. "You there--go out and break their bows and arrows." Her servants did as they were ordered. Not only did they confiscate the weapons, they chased the men away from the house.

Since it was approaching night, Granganimeo's wife urged Barlowe and his party. "You must be my guests and remain the night. It is too late for you to go back to your boat."

Barlowe and Amandas conferred. "I don't trust those Indian warriors. They may be waiting outside to attack us."

"But if we remain here, we could be murdered in our sleep," Amandas said.

"We'd better leave. Be alert." Barlowe turned to his hostess. "We appreciate your hospitality, but we must leave now."

"Dear me, it looks like rain and you not finished eating. Take this with you," she insisted and handed them a pot of food to eat later.

Some of the Indians followed the Englishmen out to their boat, then sat on the bank, comforting them and entreating them to return to the village with them. When it began to rain, the Indians paddled out to the white men's boat carrying blankets to shelter them from the storm.

It was cramped and damp in the small boat, but Barlowe wouldn't change his mind. "We are so few and they are so many. If we should be killed, the entire expedition would be in jeopardy."

Barlowe in his account to Sir Walter Raleigh bragged about how kind and loving the people were. He wrote of what a perfect place he had found to place a colony, ignoring the fact that the Outer Banks consisted mostly of sand, incapable of producing enough food to support a settlement.

Granganameo and his tribe were always at war with one tribe or another. He tried to convince Barlowe to join him in one of his wars. With the addition of the Englishmen's weapons victory would be assured. Barlowe refused. They lingered along the coast for several weeks. When they were preparing to return to England, they invited two Indians--

Manteo and Wanchese to accompany them.

ATTEMPTED SETTLEMENT

The following year another party of Englishmen under the command of Raleigh's cousin, Sir Richard Grenville, and Ralph Lane were sent to verify Barlowe's reports. The two Indians, Manteo and Wanchese, returned with them.

Queen Elizabeth didn't invest any of the government's money in the venture, but she purchased some shares with her own money. The fleet carried 108 colonists and over 500 sailors and soldiers. The large number of armed men proves their primary intent was privateering instead of colonization. They dawdled several weeks in the West Indies before proceeding to the Carolinas. This angered Lane. "We need to depart at once if we're to arrive in time to prepare for the winter."

"We'll go when I say go." Grenville prepared to make another short pirating trip.

"We were sent here to establish a colony, not to go privateering." Lane attempted to control his temper.

When they arrived at the Outer Banks it was obvious this place was not suitable for colonization. The soil was too poor to raise the crops they would need to survive. The water was too shallow near the coast for large ships to anchor, so they had to lay to far out at sea.

The leaders held a council meeting to decide their next move. "I don't know what your plans are," Grenville said, "but I intend to go pirating." His officers agreed with him.

"I was sent here to perform a specific duty. And I

intend to do it to the best of my ability. I will remain here to explore the area," Lane said. Then with a sly dig, "We might even discover some precious metals."

This was enough to persuade Grenville to tarry a few weeks. He sent a small party to the mainland with Manteo and Wanchese as guides. When they returned, Grenville determined to send four shallow draft boats with 50 men and supplies for eight days to cross the sounds. The little flotilla traveled as far north as Lake Mattamuskeet and as far south as the Neuse River and Core Sound. They built temporary forts at several places for protection against the savages.

At one place Grenville showed his arrogant behavior which turned the Indians against the colonists. He was informed that a silver cup was missing. "It was stolen by someone in that last place we visited. We will return at once and get it back."

The Indians denied any knowledge of the cup. When Grenville reached for his gun, the Indians disappeared into the woods. "I'll teach them not to steal from me." Grenville burned their corn fields and town. The people fled before him. Grenville was proud of what he had accomplished that day, but the time would come when others would regret it.

Grenville felt he was a superior being. In his opinion there were two classes of people, the quality and the scum. He considered both the Indians and his crew scum.

Most of the information concerning the Indians Grenville and Lane met on this expedition comes from artist John White's drawings and maps.

Even before visiting the mainland villages, Grenville had sent a message by Manteo to King Wingina on Roanoke

Island. They arrived on July 29th. Two days later, Chief Granganimeo, accompanied by Manteo, came aboard.

Throughout their journey, there had been dissension between Grenville and Lane, but during the next three weeks they managed to work together long enough to build a fort and shelters near the village of Wingina and Granganimeo on the north end of the island.

Grenville departed to go pirating, taking with him many of the men. Among those remaining were artist John White and the scientist Harriot. Before coming on their trip, Harriot had spent some time with Manteo and Wanchese learning their language and teaching them his. This was a great assistance when they arrived in the New World.

By the time Grenville left, it was too late in the season to plant crops. Lane was a soldier, not interested in learning to farm as the Indians did or even to catch fish as they did. He had expected to depend on the Indians for food and supplies, first by trade, then later by intimidation.

One of Lane's men who understood a little of the Indians's language, came to him with a rumor. "They say there's a giant sea to the north filled with pearls. And--now listen to this--they say there's a mountain of gold to the west."

Since Grenville had already explored to the south, Lane made little effort to learn more about that area. The only pearls they had seen were black ones, of little value, probably acquired by trading with other tribes.

The idea of pearls and gold quickened the hearts of Lane and his men. Lane wanted to see for himself. He took the pinnace, two double wherries, and other smaller vessels.

They halted at each village along the way, expecting to be provisioned. They passed through what are now the counties of Camden, Pasquotank, Perquimans, and Chowan, near rivers that flowed into Albemarle Sound.

They turned north, entering the Chowan River where they came to an Indian town Lane called the "Blind Towne." Then they arrived at the west bank of the Chowan to the village of Choanoke, a large town, capable of putting 700 fighting men into the field as well as warriors from outlying areas.

Lane was impressed by the size of this town. Menatonon, who was the king, was crippled in his body, but wise in his mind. Lane took this man and his son Skiko as prisoners so he could learn all the knowledge the man possessed about the wealth of the land.

Lane later said Menatonon gave him more information than he had acquired from anyone else. Menatonon showed him some pearls he had acquired from a powerful nation to the north east. From him he learned of an established trade route three canoe days up the Chowan River and four days overland to the bay itself.

Lane planned to search for a site for permanent settlement with a deep water harbor and find the source of the valuable pearls.

It was March when Lane took Menatonon prisoner. He was to meet Grenville less than a month away at Easter with reinforcements of both men and ships. Lane decided to wait until Grenville arrived with additional forces before allowing Menatonon to go home, Lane squeezed all the information he could get from him. "Just where is that mountain of gold you bragged about?"

Menatonon was a sly old man. He gave Lane explicit directions on how to get there. Lane's eyes lit up at the prospect of a mountain so filled with gold that it glistened in the sunlight. He set out at once. Before reaching his goal, he had to pass through territory of the Moratucks to the where the mountain was said to be located.

Lane sailed back down the calm Chowan to Albemarle Sound and began traveling up the Roanoke.

It was tough going with only oar power. Lane had made a serious mistake. He had left with food enough for only a few days, thinking he could obtain additional supplies from the Indian tribes along the way. But the Indians had been warned that these strangers coming among them were not friendly travelers but were conquerors. Occasionally Lane could see natives on the shore, but when he landed, he found the Indian villages were deserted, stripped clean of anything which might feed the starving men.

Finally when they were down to a few days' food and not having found any friendly Indians or grain, he gathered his leaders about him and said, "We have been betrayed by our own savages. We should return homeward." But his men were infected with gold fever and insisted on going ahead.

He told them to think about it overnight, and the following morning they would vote on it. They decided that while there was one-half pint of corn for every man, they would not leave off their search for the river.

"We have two large mastiff dogs. If we get desperate, I guess we can eat them," Lane said.

They pressed on against the current of the mighty

Roanoke River. When their corn was gone and they were near starvation, they heard Indians talking in the distance and stopped to listen.

Lane told Manteo to go speak with them. But before he had an opportunity to do so, the attack came, a volley of arrows hit the boats, but no one was injured.

Lane answered with gunfire. This scattered the attackers. Then they searched the woods which were deserted. Since night had fallen, they made camp ashore, putting out guards all night. They butchered the dogs. With this sustenance, they began their descent back down the Roanoke. The next day they ate nothing but a potage of sassafras leaves, seasoned with dog bones.

When they finally reached the sound, the wind was so strong there was no possibility of crossing. On Easter Sunday when they were scheduled to meet Grenville, they were at anchor. Lane later commented, "The men fasted very truly that day."

The day after Easter, they returned from their exploration, only to find Grenville had not yet arrived. They were alone in the wilderness, hungry and discouraged.

The relations between the English and the natives had been strained even before Lane had taken off on his ill-fated exploration trip. The natives could not forget the firing the fields and town because of the loss of a cup. The Indians kept in constant communication with other tribes by means of runners. Four of these young runners including Manteo had accompanied Lane on his trip west.

Later Lane said, "There was no town where we had any subtle devise practiced against us, that within a few days after our departure, the people began to die very fast."

Modern historians think this was the result of diseases brought to them by the English for which the Indians had no resistance--small pox or measles, or even colds or pneumonia.

By the time Lane returned to Roanoke, Wingina was surprised and shocked to see him return. Lane strolled past him without speaking. In his own quarters, he told his men, "That redskin planned this whole thing. We were deliberately led astray. He wanted us to die on that God-forsaken river from starvation."

Soon after Lane's return an Indian runner brought him a box of pearls. Lane was pleased and thanked him profusely.

"Now you release Skiko, prince of the Weapemeoc."

Then Lane realized the pearls were not a gift but a ransom. He refused to release Skiko.

When Wingina called his leaders together for a council, the views of his father, Ensenore, a man of peace, prevailed. The Indians set out special weirs to catch fish for the settlers and planted sufficient corn to feed Lane's company for another year. Wingina even provided a plot of land for the English to plant their own crops.

This was April and it would take months before the corn would ripen. Lane put pressure on Wingina to provide more food. But Wingina had barely enough to feed his own people. Then his father, Ensenore, died.

Menatonon's son Skiko, had been friendly with the English in spite of being kept prisoner. He told Lane, "A new plot is being hatched against you by Wanchese and Wingina. They are attempting to unite the chiefs of the various tribes in order to destroy the white intruders. They plan to weaken you until you will be unable to defend yourselves. With 700 braves from above Albemarle Sound and 700 warriors from distant tribes, 20 men will attack your house in the dead of night. Then they will fire the reeds which cover the house. When you come running out, you will be knocked in the head, and your brains bashed out."

Similar attacks were to be made against Harriot and other English leaders. All the houses and buildings in the fort were to be burned.

Lane prepared his defense. He sent men out in every direction so he could be warned when the men began to assemble. He sent word to Wingina at his new headquarters on the mainland that he planned to go to Croatan. He lied and said he had received a message that Grenville's fleet had been sighted. He asked for fish and game to feed his men for four days.

"I will go to Roanoke Island," Wingina promised. But he delayed his arrival. So Lane decided to go ahead with his own plan. He ordered his men to steal all the Indians' canoes. In doing so, they met up with a canoe going from shore. They overcame the Indians and cut off two savages' heads. A cry arose and a battle ensued. Three or four Indians were killed by the Englishmen. The remainder fled into the woods.

That night Lane crossed the sound to Wingina's camp with a force of 25 men. Wingina's messengers met Lane at the landing. He sent word he was going to Croatan, but first he wanted him to know that one of Wingina's weroances had released his prisoner Skiko.

Wingina agreed to allow Lane and he men enter the

village. Seven or eight weroances were assembled in the village. Lane sounded a prearranged signal for attack, shouting, "Christ is our victory!" His soldiers opened fire. Wingina was struck by gunfire and fell to the ground as if dead. But when Lane's back was turned, Wingina leapt to his feet and took off to the woods.

Lane's personal servant, an Irishman named Nugent, overtook the king. Soon Nugent returned carrying the king's bloody head.

Wingina, king of the Roanokes, was dead by the Irishman's hands. The one who had welcomed the English to their shores, had been betrayed and destroyed by the ones he had gone out of his way to befriend.

Grenville ran into difficulty trying to put together the relief effort. At Easter, when he was supposed to meet Lane at Roanoke, he hadn't even left England. When he learned of the problems, Raleigh arranged to send a small relief ship with adequate supplies to tide the stranded colonists over until the main force would arrive.

But another English fleet was closer at hand.

Sir Francis Drake, pirate and privateer, sailed close to the Outer Banks. When Lane heard of his arrival, he hurriedly traveled towards the shore, where he arranged passage for himself and his men back to the safety of England. After killing Wingina, there was no place where he and his men would be safe along the coast of Carolina.

WHITE MEN WERE GODS

Thomas Harriot, who was a member of Raleigh's Second Expedition to coastal Carolina, wrote about the land, plants, animals, and Indians he found there. He also discussed the native's religion and the explorers' attempt to convert them to the English religion.

Harriot said he learned much from their priests, some of whom were not firmly grounded in their own faith. After talking to him, some began to doubt their beliefs and accept the white man's faith.

The compasses, magnets, spyglasses, magnifying glasses, fireworks, guns, hooks, and writing and reading materials the English brought with them convinced the Indians the white men were gods.

"It was rather uncomfortable being considered as a god," Harriot wrote. "I told them there is only one God, the god of the Bible. The people reverenced the Bible, thought it magic and wanted to touch it, embrace it, and kiss it."

Wingina and his people joined the English at prayers and tried to sing with them. At two different times when Wingina became seriously ill, he called for Harriot to come pray with him. "I want to live, but if I cannot, I want to dwell with Him in bliss."

Others who became ill asked for the same prayers.

The Indians said, "Our corn dies because we displease white men. Let us ask them to forgive us and pray for our corn. We share it with them when it becomes ripe."

They believed their illness came because they had displeased the white men, that if they wished to remain healthy, they must provide them with food. Harriot did nothing to discourage this belief.

Some Indians came to Harriot. "We want the power you have, the power to make our enemies ill like white man do."

"That power comes not from us but from God. You must pray for this power and help the white man when he asks," Harriot said.

When their enemies became sick, they believed they too had the power to make them ill.

When some people who lived in the towns near the Englishmen also became sick, the Indians claimed the white men could send their illnesses without even seeing their victims. An eclipse of the sun the previous year and a comet while they were there further added to their fear of the Englishmen.

Wingina prophesied to his tribe, "More of these strange creatures will come to kill the people and take away our lands. They not human but gods from another time."

The Indians believed in many gods of different sorts and degrees.

Harriot said, "There is only one God. He created the sun, moon, and stars, the waters and the animals. But they are not gods, just God's creation."

"The gods made the waters first and out of the water the gods made all creatures. A woman was the first human made. She was made pregnant by one of the lesser gods, and children were born," Wingina insisted.

Harriot didn't want to argue, but he felt he had to set him straight. "Our Bible says that the first man, Adam, was created by God. Then He made a wife for Adam from his rib. He called her Eve."

"Aw, your God is a conjurer." A grin spread across the Indian's face. "We have many gods, some have human shapes."

"There is only one God, God Almighty. Then there is His Son, Jesus Christ."

"You say there is only one God, yet you say there are two." Wingina thought he understood. "Is because your God is a conjurer."

While Harriot was trying to decide how to explain this, Wingina went on with another story.

"One man who had died claimed his soul has come very near entering into Popogusso [Hell]. One of the gods saved him and gave him leave to return again to teach his friends what they should do to avoid that terrible place of torment. Does your Bible tell of this man?"

So Harriot told him of the rich man who went to Hell and wanted to come back so he could warn his friends of that place. And Harriot told him about Lazarus, the one who had risen from the grave.

"We have the same story. Although his body was dead and buried, his soul was alive. It traveled a long, broad way between delicate and pleasant trees, bearing rare and excellent fruits. At length he came to most brave and fair houses, near which he met his father that had been dead before, who gave him great charge to go back again and show his friends what good they were to do if they wanted to go to this great place."

Harriot described Hell as a place of ever-lasting

burning fire. But the Indian objected. "No, no--Hell is a place of cold and hunger and ugly women."

"And what of Heaven?" Harriot asked, attempting to conceal his amusement.

"Heaven is a land of abundance and contentment. Of eternal youth and good hunting where every month is May. And the women are bright as stars and never scold."

Harriot puzzled over Wingina's religion, so like, yet so different than his own. Where had his ideas come from? It was almost as if generations ago, Christian missionaries had come to this place and through countless re-telling of the story, it became garbled. So he told Wingina about Jesus Christ and the salvation He offered.

THE RESCUE

On June 18, 1586 Lane left with Drake's fleet. Because of his hasty departure, he left three of his men behind.

Even as they were leaving, a relief vessel was on its way with supplies. Since it had left London in early April, it should have arrived there even before Lane left with his men.

The captain of this ship wrote, "Lane left all things in confusion, as if chased from thence by mighty armies. The hand of God came upon them because of the cruelty and outrages committed against the native inhabitants of the country."

After a few days spent searching for traces of the missing Lane colonists, they turned around and returned to England.

Many have debated the wisdom of this captain. He had

spent months preparing for this trip to the New World, so why did he return to England with the same supplies, knowing all the while that Grenville was close behind him? Perhaps the evidence of Lane's hasty departure frightened him so that he feared for his own safety.

Fourteen or 15 days after the first rescue ship left, Grenville arrived with three vessels. He had left England in late April, but as usual, took time to go pirating. Had he arrived on time to rescue Lane's company, the fate of the English colony might have been different.

Grenville anchored off the north end of Hatteras Island, then headed in a small boat for Roanoke Island. There he found the fort and settlement deserted except for the body of one Englishman who had been hanged and a dead Indian.

Grenville then sailed up the coast and into the sounds and rivers searching for some clue as to what had happened to Lane and his colonists. In one place they found three Indians they took prisoner. Two of them escaped, but when questioned the other one said, "Big ships come. Lane and his men go with them."

"Did they go willingly or were they forced?"

"Men ran like deer escaping hunter's arrows." From the Indian's description of the ships, Grenville realized it was Sir Francis Drake who had rescued the colonists.

So now what should he do? Re-establish the colony, leaving behind some of the men he had brought with him from England? Or forget the whole affair and go back to England as he had come?

Unwilling to give up England's claim to the country, Grenville finally decided to leave behind 15 men and sufficient supplies to last them for two years. Then he returned to England to report to Sir Walter Raleigh and Queen Elizabeth.

THE LOST COLONY

Even though Lane and his men had left in fear of their lives, Queen Elizabeth went ahead with her plans to send another group, including women, to the New World. John White was appointed governor of the Fourth Expedition and Ferdinando captain of the fleet. Some records claim there were 150 colonists but only 121 names were recorded.

At it had been with the Second Expedition, there were serious altercations between the two leaders. While stopping off in the West Indies for water and fresh supplies, Fernando sent his men off on a false search for salt.

"He's gone chasing after women while time's wasting. We should be at Raleigh by now," John White complained.

At last they were headed for Carolina. On July 16, 1587 land was sighted. White shouted at Ferdinando, "You incompetent ass! You have deceived us. This is not Cape Hatteras. We are miles from there."

It was true.

"I believe we are near that dreaded Cape Fear, the place noted for its shipwrecks," Captain Stafford said as he studied the map. He watched all night, sensitive to the danger of sand bars and shallow water. His vigilance prevented the ship from adding to the fabled wrecks off Cape Fear. Raleigh had ordered, "When you arrive at Virginia [Carolina] before going to the location chosen for your new settlement north at Chesapeake Bay, stop over at Roanoke to check on the 15 men left there by Grenville."

White was anxious about the brave men left to survive among the Indians. After the way Lane had abused the savages, he doubted if any of them remained alive. On the other hand, if they were alive and well, it portended good luck for his own venture. He planned to meet with them, then go with the fleet along the coast to Chesapeake as Raleigh had ordered to establish a permanent settlement.

But no sooner had White and 40 of his men crowded aboard the pinnace to go ashore, than Ferdinando shouted to his men, "Don't allow any of the planters to return to the ship except the governor and two or three men of his choosing."

"Why? Raleigh's orders were to look for those 15 men here, then to proceed on to the new location at Chesapeake." White could barely be civil to the man.

"You are to be put off here on the island. It is far too late in the season to start a new settlement elsewhere," Ferdinando said.

One of the problems with both the Lane and the White settlements seems to be the overabundance of arrogant leaders. Since Ferdinando was in charge of the ships and White of the land, Ferdinando was within his rights to put them ashore. He dumped the colonists and their belongings on the deserted beach, then took off to go pirating.

At the site of the former settlement they found no signs of the 15 men left there by Lane.

The next morning they searched the rest of the island, but found no sign of the missing men. The fort was gone, but the houses remained. It was obvious that no one had lived there since winter because the lower floors of the two-storied buildings were overgrown with melons and gourds. Deer wandered unafraid feeding on the melons.

So they returned to their company, without hope of seeing any of the 15 men.

Later they met a lone Indian in the woods, who explained the mystery. "Two men came to the group of white men. No weapons. One embraced a white man to show love. Other man drew club from under coat. Hit white man on head, kill him. Other Indians came out of bushes. Attack. White men foolish. Hide in house. Indians set it afire. Men run outside. White men stand and fight. Indians hide behind trees. Shoot. All white men killed but four, who in sound oystering. They flee to small island near Hatteras. No see them since."

White accepted this as truth. The cottages were repaired and new cottages built, thus establishing the city of Raleigh.

During the first few days on the island, no other Indians were seen, giving the colonists a false sense of security. Then George Howe, one of White's 12 assistants, decided to go crabbing alone. He took off his shirt and waded out into the water, leaving his weapons on shore, carrying only a forked stick. A group of Indians appeared from the reeds. They fell upon the defenseless man, delivering 16 wounds with arrows. Then they beat him upon the head with wooden swords until they killed him, his head split open like a squashed melon.

The attackers, who were a remnant of Wingina's men, escaped with Wanchese over the water to the mainland.

Wanchese, unlike Manteo, seems to have harbored resentment at being taken to England and turned against the English.

On July 30th Captain Stafford led a group of men by water to the Island of Croatan [what is now Core and Shackleford Banks], where Hatteras Indians met them. "They look hostile to me," Stafford told his lieutenant.

Manteo, who had remained true to the English, called to the Indians in their own language. "It's all right. We are friends. Throw away your bows and arrows."

The meeting was cordial. The Indians prepared a feast for the colonists. Then they asked Manteo to say, "There is little corn in the fields. They beg you promise not to gather or spoil their fields, for grain is scarce."

"We do not want to harm your corn fields," Stafford said. "We come only to make peace and friendship."

"We ask for some sort of badge or mark so that you will know we are your friends. When Lane was here, he hurt some of our men," Manteo translated.

At a council held the next day, it was proposed that the Croatan send a runner with a message of forgiveness to the near-by tribes, asking the chiefs of these tribes for pledges of friendship.

"We will gladly send such messages and return to you within seven days along with the chiefs of these tribes for a conference," they said.

So the colonists returned to Roanoke Island to await the arrival of the chiefs.

The time came and went when they should have come. As the days passed, Governor White became impatient. "We have been deceived once again by these thieving redskins. It's pay back time."

That night White with a party of 25 men went to the mainland. In the darkness of a moonless night, they attacked a band of Indians camped on shore. The Indians fled into clumps of reeds, leaving one dead Indian behind.

At dawn White discovered he had made a tragic mistake. The men he had attacked were friendly Indians, come to gather the crops Wingina's men had deserted when they ran away after killing George Howe.

Manteo was disturbed about what had happened, "It was partly my fault. But I had no way of knowing who they were. They should have reported to the governor on the appointed day."

"Well, as long as we're here," John White said, "we might as well gather the corn, peas, pumpkins, and tobacco." So they collected that which was ripe, leaving the remainder in the fields.

On August 13th, as a reward for his many services, Manteo was christened, "Lord of Roanoke and of Dasamonquepeuk." The following week Virginia Dare, the first white child born in America, was christened. She was the daughter of Ananias and Eleanor Dare and granddaughter of John White.

It was decided to send a ship back to England to ask for more supplies and reinforcements. John White took two pages in his report to Sir Walter Raleigh to explain why (after spending only one month there) he deserted his colony and returned to England, protesting that the colonists begged him to go to arrange for more supplies. It is interesting to note that before he left, he had the colonists sign a paper guaranteeing the preservation of his belongings.

Now both leaders of the expedition were gone.

John White, who had returned to England in June of 1587 to arrange for additional supplies for the colonists, made efforts to return to the New World. However because of the political situation and possibility of war with Spain, it was not until March of 1590 that such a journey was undertaken.

White was little more than a passenger on board one of the ships. After spending most of the summer plundering Spaniards to the south, they were in the 34th latitude, a few miles north of Cape Fear. Towards night they were within three leagues of islands west of Wocokon [Ocracoke]. The second latitude recorded is 35 degrees, also west of Wocokon.

Apparently White didn't know where he was on this journey. He was to lead the ships to where the colonists had been left three years earlier, but he was not a navigator or pilot or even a seaman. He was an artist and map maker.

"Are you certain this is the right place?" the captain asked.

Before White could answer, the vessel hit a submerged object and men were thrown overboard. Several men were lost at sea.

"I see a fire in the North Woods," White shouted above the crashing sea. "Praise the Lord, they must be alive!" Since it was now dark, they used the fire to guide them to the North Woods. In order to attract the attention of the colonists, they blew a trumpet and sang familiar songs. White

called out his daughter's name, "Eleanor! Eleanor!"

But no one answered.

When dawn came, they landed. All they found was a burned out grass fire surrounded by Indian moccasin prints in the sand. They searched the north end of the island, trying to find some trace of the colonists. Where White said the houses should be there was nothing but woods.

Bark had been skinned from one of the main trees at the right side of where White said the entrance should be. Five feet above the ground the word CROATAN was carved.

The only trace of the colonists were bars of iron, pigs of lead, and heavy shot scattered around. Five chests, three of which were White's, had been broken open. "My books, my pictures, my maps and armor, they're all ruined. And they promised me they would protect my belongings."

"Did you hear that man? He's crazy. He seems more concerned about his belongings than his missing daughter and granddaughter," one man said to another.

White overheard them. "I know my daughter is safe with the Croatan Indians."

"We're returning to England, and that's that," the captain announced.

So the colonists were once again deserted to their fate. And what was that fate? This question has troubled historians for over four hundred years. There are three possibilities:

They were all killed.

Some married Indian women and scattered about the different tribes around Chesapeake Bay and Croatan.

They remained in the area.

Entire books have been devoted to answering this

question. There were at least 100 men, women and children from White's settlement as well as 14 whose bodies were never found from Lane's Expedition.

An official letter dated September 10, 1606 found in Spain, states: "Peccarecamicke where you shall find four of the English alive, left by Sir Walter Raleigh which escaped from the slaughter of Powhaton of Roanoke, upon the first arrival of our Colony, and live under the protection of a Wiroane called Gepanocon enemy to Powhaton, by whose consent you shall never recover them. One of these were worth much labor, and if you find them not yet search into this country, it is more probable than toward the north."

After Jamestown was settled, attempts were made to locate the lost colonists, George Percy described an expedition into the Virginia interior. "At Port Cottage in our voyage up the river, we saw boy of about 10 years with yellow hair and white skin."

He also spoke of white men who lived in the Back Bay.

He described a country he called Anone where they had an abundance of brass and houses built like the English. The expedition sent to investigate was led by men too frightened of the Indians to make an adequate search.

Many historians believe the so-called Lost Colonists went north to Chesapeake Bay where they were originally scheduled to settle.

Sir Walter Raleigh had almost lost interest in colonizing America, but 15 years after his colony had been abandoned, since his grant was about to expire, he sent a ship to investigate. Because of bad weather, they did not make land and returned to England.

For years many have believed that some of the colonists joined with Manteo's tribe on Croatan and later moved to what is now Lumberton, North Carolina. [More about this will be discussed at greater length later.]

Possibly some of the colonists remained in the same general area. The way of speaking resembles that of the old English. Several names of those on the list of the colonists appears in these areas.

There are so many tales of people wearing white man's clothes, living in white man's houses, and using white man's utensils, that we have to agree that some of these Lost Colonists did survive.

JOHN LEDERER

John Lederer, a German doctor, was often called the father of the Piedmont explorers. On May 20, 1670, he marched westward from the James River in Virginia with Major Harris, 20 men on horseback, and five Indians.

On June 5th Harris and everyone except Lederer and Jackzetavon, an Indian guide, turned back in fear of the savages. Four days later Lederer and his guide arrived at the Indian town of Saxony, south of present Lynchburg.

Here the Indians gave Lederer a warm welcome. The king presented Lederer with a beautiful young woman. "My daughter. She be your wife." And he grinned with pleasure.

For a moment, Lederer couldn't answer. He couldn't accept this woman, but he didn't want to insult his host. Then he spoke with gratitude, "What a welcome gift. She will make an admirable wife. There is only one problem. I must go on my way at this time, but I will return in six months to consummate the marriage." So upon this promise, they allowed him safe passage.

He had no intention of again passing that way.

The next town they reached was Occaneechee, a well-fortified settlement with abundant crops of corn. The tribe was ruled by two chiefs, one for peace and the other for war. According to Lederer, they held all things in common except their wives. When they ate, the entertainer sat between the two chiefs. After the entertainer and chiefs had eaten until they were satisfied, the remainder of the company were allowed to eat.

On the day after Lederer's arrival, several important guests arrived from beyond the Blue River. Tribal dancing followed the feast. In the midst of the festivities, the lodge was darkened. Lederer hid beneath his seat. Screams filled the air, as the guests were attacked and murdered.

Lederer located his guide and drew him aside. "We'd best leave before they decide to kill us next." They lay awake in terror until they were certain their hosts were sleeping soundly, then slipped away unnoticed.

Lederer wrote of the Eno Indians, not far from the present Hillsboro. "This town was built around a field which was used for sports. The ground was soaked from the sweat of the contestants."

According to Lederer, these Indians were atypical. "They were mean of stature and courage, covetous, thievery, and so industrious to earn money they even hired themselves out as porters or carriers." They planted three crops of grain a year. Their houses were built of wailing and plaster, generally round. They parched nuts and acorns over the fire to take away their oiliness, then pressed them to provide an oil they used to dip their cakes into for a treat. The government was democratic in nature, and the words of the old men were reverenced.

In what is now Randolph County, Lederer found the Watary [Wateree] Indians. Here he said, "The king is a monarch and the people, slaves."

The king was in mourning because of the death of his son. He called three young braves before him, "Go kill as many young women as possible to serve my son in the other world."

Because of the king's inhumanity, Lederer was

concerned about his own safety. He wanted to leave, but the king would not allow it.

A few days later, Lederer was horrified when the youths returned and presented the king with the skin which had been torn off the heads and faces of three young girls. The king gratefully received this offering for his dead son.

In the midst of the celebration, Lederer and his guide slipped away unobserved.

At a settlement near the present site of Ashboro, he came upon Uwharrie, where the Indians came to obtain minerals to make war paint. Near here, some young boys with bows and arrows used Lederer's horse for target practice. The adult Indians were amused, but Lederer wasn't. He rescued his horse and sped away, but not before an arrow whizzed past his ear.

Of the Catawba, he said, "They use many feathers as ornaments. The men are handsome, effeminate and lazy, filled with illusions of the devil." One man stood barefoot for nearly an hour on burning coals. Lederer's guide turned his head away, unable to observe the man's scorching feet.

To Lederer's surprise, the man leaped from the fire. He examined the man's feet, then shook his head in disbelief. "There is no sign of burns," he told his guide.

"There are men such as you who live to the southwest," the king said. From his description, Lederer deduced they were Spaniards. He didn't want to test his welcome among them. Since he knew the war-like Cherokee were to the northwest, he decided to go towards the east.

Soon he was once again in familiar territory.

NEEDHAM & ARTHUR

In 1673, three years after Lederer's trip, Abraham Wood [a trader from Fort Henry, Virginia] wanted to discover more about the possibilities of opening a new trade route to the Indians in the back country.

He chose James Needham, a gentleman of some means to lead the expedition. He was accompanied by a talented, but ignorant boy named Gabriel Arthur, and 10 Virginia Indians. On the way they met a party of Tomahitan Indians who agreed to guide them to the west.

They arrived at the island home of the Occaneechee. These Indians were an influential tribe. Since traders had to pass through their island gateway to reach the west, and the westward traders had to pass through to reach the trade with the east, they controlled all back country trade. Because of this, they were prosperous.

They refused to allow the Virginia Indians to pass through, so Needham and Arthur left, accompanied by only one Appomattox Indian. They traveled nine days west and south, crossing many rivers and creeks over the Old Trading Path before they spied the Great Smoky Mountains on their right.

At the end of 15 days, they arrived at the Tomahitan town. Only the two white men and one horse survived the journey. These Indians had never seen a horse before, so they were curious at this strange beast. Since the natives appeared friendly, Needham felt it was safe enough to leave young Arthur there while he returned to Virginia.

"While I am gone, you are to learn the language of the natives so that we may understand them to trade with them. I will be back as soon as I can after reporting to Mr. Wood."

Abraham Wood was pleased at Needham's report. On September 20th, he sent him back, accompanied by 20 Tomahitans, who had come with him.

Wood waited in vain for a report from Needham. He grew more and more concerned when no word arrived. He considered sending another party out to look for him, but decided to wait, lest he lose more men.

Toward the last of January, rumors came that Needham had been killed by the Tomahitan. Other rumors came, verifying this fact.

In February, Henry Hatcher, an English trader reported to Wood. "I was at Occaneechee when Needham asked them for permission to continue his journey west. It was only at my interference that he was allowed to pass. Needham was killed soon after he left. The Occaneechee says that it was Indian John, one of Needham's Tomahitan Indians who killed him. He had Needham's pistols and gun, so it had to be true."

Gabriel Arthur returned to Virginia in June. He reported to Wood. "Needham and his party were crossing the Uwharrie River, when Indian John, an Occaneechee Indian, dropped his pack into the water. 'You clumsy oaf,' Needham said. From this, they began arguing. They fussed all day until they reached Yadkin Town.

"Indian John continued to argue until finally, Needham seized his sword and threw his hatchet upon the ground, challenging Indian John to a fight. Indian John, not allowing him to defend himself, grabbed a rifle and fired a bullet into Needham's head, killing him. Before the Tomahitan Indians could rescue him, Indian John grabbed a knife, ripped open the chest of the dead man, and tore out his heart. He held it high, facing the east, cursing at the English."

"Were you there?"

"No. I came later with the Tomahitan chief and 18 others of that tribe, laden with furs. When we reached the scene, we could see some of Needham's possessions scattered about on the ground. As we attempted to gather them up, we were surprised by four Occaneechee waiting for us. We ran and hid in some bushes.

"We remained hidden until they gave up searching for us. The next morning, we continued on our way."

So the mystery of Needham was solved.

JOHN LAWSON'S JOURNEY

John Lawson was from London, a gentleman by birth, well-educated, cultured, and wealthy. He was a writer, surveyor, ethologist, geologist, botanist, and map maker. He was many things, but probably his most important attribute was his ability to listen. He traveled among the Indians, and everywhere he went, he learned from them.

He came to Carolina about 1700 to work as a surveyor, assisting in settling the long disputed boundary line between North Carolina and Virginia. Shortly after his arrival, he obtained land in the Pamlico area along the banks of Old Town Creek [now Bath Creek]. Lawson laid out the plan for the town of Bath, where he became active in the political and economic life of the town. He aided Baron de Graffenried in the purchase of land and establishment of the town of New Bern.

Lawson took a 1,000 mile journey among the Indian tribes of both Carolinas, studying their way of life, language, and relationship with the white men and other tribes.

He began in a great canoe at Charles Town in South Carolina. His company consisted of six English men, three Indian men, and the wife of the Indian guide. He carried some supplies, but he expected to trade with the Indians for what they needed along the way. By canoe and by foot, he traveled from one tribe to another, hiring guides as he went. Lawson didn't try to preach to the Indians. He traded with them, but mostly he learned. He observed the way they lived, cooked and thought. Because of this, he was made welcome almost everywhere he went.

Many books have been written about the various tribes he visited, their structure, location, and language. But more interesting are the stories he told concerning them and the other inhabitants of the area.

THE ALLIGATOR

Lawson says that the alligator is like the crocodile except in name. They make their homes in the sides of rivers. The monster sleeps away during the winter months and only comes out of his cave when spring comes. He swims up and down the stream daily. He doesn't eat men--at least not in Carolina, but instead avoids them whenever possible. He kills swine when they come to feed in the marshes and sometimes dogs as they swim over the creeks and waters.

An alligator often exceeds 17 feet in length. Lawson claims it is impossible to kill one of them with a gun, unless you happen to hit it about the eyes. In bad weather, they roar and make a hideous noise. He knows this because of what he experienced.

When he first arrived in the area, he built a house about a half mile from an Indian town on the Forks of the Neuse River. He lived there by himself except for a young Indian servant and a bull dog.

One night in March, Lawson was alone sitting by the fireside with only his dog as company, since his Indian servant had gone to town to visit with his family. "Suddenly I heard such a roaring, it set the whole house shaking about

my ears. My dog slunk under the table, too scared to even bark." Lawson wrote, "I began to think the Indians were working some sort of conjure on my house to get away with my goods."

Lawson was too frightened to go outside to see what the noise was all about. It was a long night, but, at last his servant returned. When Lawson related his story, his servant laughed. "It was only an alligator. He has his nest directly under the house. He's as afraid of you as you are of him."

Lawson says, "An alligator's tail, when cut off looks very fair and white, like the best of veal. People who have eaten it say it is a delicate meat. They also say that after the tail of the alligator has been separated from the body, it will move about freely for four days."

SANTEES AND THE POX

Things went well with Lawson's journey. Several days out, they arrived at the first Santee town. The Santees were located along the Santee River in South Carolina. Once they had a population of 1,000 to 1,600 people, but since the English arrived, their number had rapidly decreased.

Lawson blamed this upon the "pox." He observed that not only the Sewees [Santees], but the other nations as well, suffered from this same malady.

Since the Indians had no natural immunity, the European diseases, especially small-pox, destroyed thousands of the natives.

When they were attacked with the violent fever, to ease the high temperatures, they flung themselves into water, completely covering their heads. Lawson claims that at the height of the disease, this shuts up the pores and hinders the natural evacuation of the pestilential matter [sweating out the disease], driving it back in, causing death.

But in other diseases, the Indian medicine men were skilled and quite successful in their cures. Often they traveled far to collect the roots, barks, berries, nuts, and leaves for needed nostrums. Medicine men carried their drugs strung on a thread hung around the neck like a "Pomander."

The Santees told Lawson of an Englishman who was a man of great wealth and who possessed many slaves. He contracted the "distemper." Several doctors and ships' surgeons were called in to treat the man. Each doctor charged him large sums until the poor man had no slaves left, but he still had the distemper.

Then Jack, an Indian who occasionally stayed with the

planter, visited him again. When Jack saw the condition of his host, he was shocked. "Brother, I can see that you long time sick. If you had called upon me when sickness come, I could have easy healed you. You would still have servants and corn to feed your family."

"But can you cure me now?"

"What you are afflicted with is Indian disease. To cure Indian disease, you need Indian physician. For English diseases, English doctors cure you. Yes, I can cure. You give me blanket to keep me warm and powder and shot to kill deer, I try to make you well."

The planter was not confident of his ability. "Jack, if our English doctors could not cure me, surely you cannot."

But the planter's wife scolded her husband, "It might be that Jack is right. If it is an Indian disease, perhaps he can cure it. After all he is asking so little, it cannot make you any poorer than you already are."

So finally to avoid listening to his nagging wife, the planter agreed. Jack went into the woods. He returned a short time later with a basket of herbs and roots. From these he prepared a concoction. As it stewed, the aroma filled the house.

He forced the planter to drink every drop. "Go to your bed and remain there until I return," he said as he left.

Almost immediately the man began sweating profusely. His wife rushed into the room. "What is that awful smell?" When she saw the sweat rolling off her husband, she went to him with a towel to soak up the perspiration. Then she realized that the offensive odor was—it was her husband. Gagging, she toweled him dry, then left him alone.

About nightfall, Jack returned with a large live rattlesnake cradled in his arms.

The planter rose from his sick bed to get away from the snake. But Jack protested, "He no harm you. You must take him to bed with you."

"Never! I'd as soon die of the distemper as be killed by the bite of that serpent."

"He no harm you. See, I remove his poison-teeth." And he showed him that they were indeed gone. He put the snake around the sick man's waist, then covered him up and ordered, "Nobody is to take away the snake on any account." Jack left the old couple alone. "I be back on the morrow."

The snake girded the planter tighter than any belt he had ever worn. The man suffered the pain in silence. He was beginning to believe this Indian knew what he was doing. Gradually the snake's twitches grew weaker and weaker, until at last the planter could not feel the snake at all. Drawing back the covers, he discovered that the snake was dead. The planter no longer felt ill, but he remained in bed until Jack returned the next morning.

"See, your distemper is dead along with the snake. It took your illness upon itself."

The man speedily recovered his strength and became perfectly well. He observed, "God has furnished every country with the specific remedies needed for their peculiar diseases."

The next morning, Lawson and his party proceeded on their way. About noon, they came upon another Santee settlement. Some of the inhabitants came out to greet them.

Since one of Lawson's party was acquainted with the Indians, they welcomed Lawson and his men.

They watched as the women prepared a fat venison to stew. They tore hunks of it in pieces with their teeth, then put it into a mortar and beat it into rags. Then it was ready to stew with water and other ingredients. Lawson said, "It made a very savory dish."

The next day the King of the Santee Nation came for a visit, bringing with him their Chief Doctor or Physician, clothed in a warm garment made of turk feathers.

"This doctor, he has no nose," the novice explorer whispered to Lawson.

The conjurer overheard and answered, "I lost my nose because of the pox."

"How did this happen?"

Lawson interrupted, "English traders brought the pox to the Indians."

But the conjurer disagreed. "Our nation has been afflicted with a disease similar to the Lues Venerea [venereal disease] for many generations, long before the white man came."

After talking to the conjurer and other people--both native and English--Lawson arrived at the conclusion that the disease began with the Indians, and after traveling around the world, returned to the Indians. [The problem seems to be that they are confusing small pox and gonorrhea, which are two separate diseases, neither one believed to have been native with the Indians.]

Lawson says that the English traders were blamed for bringing the pox to the Indians, but this particular Indian conjurer said it wasn't so.

"The disease begins with gonorrhea. Then comes night

pains in the limbs and covers the body with blotches and ulcers. Sometimes mercurial unguents and remedies work a cure, but more often the afflicted man loses his palate and nose from this disease."

Lawson was convinced that the pox came from immoderate drinking of rum by those who normally drink water, sleeping in cold rooms, open houses, or more often by wetting the feet, and eating large quantities of pork, "which," he said, "is a gross food."

Mainly he blames the change of climate for this problem.

Lawson studied on this matter and decided, "The pox began with the Indians in the New World. Columbus' men consorted with the Indian women and caught it, taking it home to Spain. The Spaniards took the pains to bring it in their breeches as far as from America, and the large consumption of pork the army victualed on, made the pox rage. Spanish soldiers went to the relief of Naples, besieged by the French. Since there were so many useless people there, and the provisions were in short supply, they were turned out of the city, especially the courtesans who had recently embraced the Spaniards.

"After the Spanish were not available, the courtesans entertained the French, taking with them the disease. The Spaniards and French retreated to Flanders where all nations met. By this means the filthy distemper scattered to most nations of the world."

Before Lawson and his party left, he said, "The King presented me with an odoriferous balsamic root, whose odor and taste were unfamiliar to me. By taking it in the mouth and

and taste were unfamiliar to me. By taking it in the mouth and chewing it, patients were healed of belly-aches and desperate wounds."

RESPECT

When Lawson's party entered an Indian town, they were welcomed by the chief king, then the war captain, and on down the line according to their status. When an aged man spoke, no Indian ever interrupted him. Instead they listened respectfully to what he had to say and did not comment until he was finished.

Lawson said, "It is almost impossible to find a scolding woman. If they are provoked by their husbands or some one else, they burst into tears or else refuse to eat."

Then he adds, "If our European daughters followed this example, life would be more peaceful."

The Indians had no written history, but they had an extensive oral history. In each tribe, at least one man kept the stories of the former days alive by repeating it so the older ones would not forget, and the younger ones would learn.

One night while gathered around the bonfire, the most aged man spoke. "Before the white man came, the People's life and needs were simple. We had all we needed to survive. The animals in the woods gave their lives that we might live. The waters our gods provided, teemed with fishes and with clams. The trees provided us with shelter and fire.

"But when the white man came, everything changed. They brought with them their own goods, cloth already prepared, pots made, and metal for tools. Ancient crafts were forgotten when the People learned they could obtain these products without laboring over them. Life was easier, but the white man cheated the Indian. The goods he brought were not of equal value to the skins he demanded. The people became dependent upon the whites to furnish them with these goods. The people became so dependent upon them, they would fight to obtain them. Before this, the Indians did not go to war except for honor or revenge. The white man has destroyed our lives."

Lawson listened and pondered on what he had heard. What the old man said was probably true of some unscrupulous traders, but surely not of himself.

THE "WINCHESTER WEDDING"

About eight o'clock the next night, Lawson's party came to a fairly large town where they found quarters in one of the state houses. They were informed that the men were all out hunting, only the women remained at home.

For some time, Lawson and his men had been teasing a fellow traveler, who had been loudly lusting for an Indian lass for a bed-fellow. Sensing a good opportunity, the Indian guide soon found two women, one for himself and one for the lusty young man.

The horny fellow's girl was young and pretty. He couldn't understand a word she said, but he soon understood her. She, although young, was apparently well-versed in the art of love. She made him understand what she expected, as Lawson said,"Pay for hire before he rode the hackney."

The young traveler showed her all the treasure he

owned; a red coat, beads, and a knife. She liked them well enough. She put the beads and knife in his coat pocket and returned the coat to him, signifying that she would come to him, not for pay, but for love.

Nothing could have enchanted him more. So it was agreed that they would mate. A group of Indian women came in from other houses to celebrate what they called the "Winchester Wedding."

"The bridesmaids were big whores, as was Mrs. Bride, but not as beautiful," Lawson said. "The happy couple went to bed before us all, and with a little blushing, as if they had been man and wife for seven years."

The rest of the company were exhausted with travel and went to bed early, not desiring to marry even though other "virgins" offered themselves.

About an hour before daybreak, Lawson awoke aware that someone was walking up and down, up and down, as if deeply disturbed. He called out, "Who is it?"

It was Mr. Bridegroom. "What's your problem? Didn't Mrs. Bride take to your love making?"

"Apparently not. When I woke, desiring her once again, I reached out, but she wasn't there. Neither was my red coat with all my possessions in the pockets."

Lawson didn't know whether to laugh at his friend's predicament or to commensurate with him.

The bridegroom was almost crying. "Worst of all, she took my shoes." He had made them the night before of dressed buckskin, and they were fine moccasins. Now he was barefoot. After the Indians woke up and heard the news, they laughed until their sides hurt. Lawson found him another pair of shoes, and he and his party resumed their journey.

But ever so often, one of the company would break out with an impassioned prayer for the happiness of the New Bridegroom and his Bride, while his mates roared with laughter

So Lawson says, "In less than 12 hours, he was a bachelor, husband, and widower, his dear spouse having picked his pocket of his possessions."

THE AGED SQUAW

At the cabin of a man named Cassetta, Lawson reported on "the strangest spectacle of antiquity I ever saw." He guessed at the age of an old woman who lived there as "over one hundred. Her face was as if in swaddling cloths. Her skin hung in reaves like a bag of tripe."

In fact, according to Lawson, she had sufficient skin to hold three persons of her size. One of her hands had been shriveled by coming in contact with fire. Since the Indians always slept as close to fire as possible, getting burned was a common occurrence. Often when the Indians were drunk, they stumbled into the fire with tragic consequences.

Lawson asked Cassetta, "How old is she?" indicating the old squaw.

"Her actual age is not known, but she is considerably over 100."

"To what does she attribute her advanced age?"

"She smokes her pipe and eats like an 18 year-old."

Lawson wondered at her longevity. The young man of the "Winchester Wedding" spoke the language of Cassetta. He wanted to make friends with one of the Indian lasses, but they would have no part of him.

The Queen and the old squaw smoked tobacco in pipes, whose bowls were carved out of stone, each containing about an ounce of tobacco. That night the men slept in King Cassetta's cabin with the Queen and the old squaw. The horny one was greatly disappointed.

They arose early the next morning, eager to be on their way. The man they had hired to be their guide, was still sleeping. "The Indians never want to set forth until the sun is an hour or two in the sky," Lawson complained.

The Queen gave them a good breakfast in spite of the constant crying of her young child. "She has colic," the mother said. To ease the child, she took some liquid already mixed in a gourd into her own mouth, then squirted it into the child's mouth, which seemed to ease the colic.

After they had eaten, they set out on their journey with their new guide.

GREAT HUNTER

Lawson's party passed over a swamp to arrive at the house of the man he wished to see. After the usual amenities, Lawson said, "We are in need of a guide, and I've been informed you are available."

"I am not a guide, I am a great hunter," he said. He was a tall man, about seven foot, much esteemed by his King for his hunting abilities. He showed Lawson the artificial deer head he used for hunting. It was made from the head of a buck, the back part of the horns scraped away to lighten the weight. The skin was left on and supported so as to look like a deer. Even the eyes appeared alive. He wore a match-coat made of deer skin with the hair left on.

The hunter placed the head on his shoulders and pranced about like a deer. "If I didn't know better, I would swear you are a deer," Lawson said.

"A friend of mine went out hunting with his brother, wearing his deer costume. He looked so real, his brother shot him, thinking him a red deer.

Since they were still in need of a guide, they left to proceed on their way, hoping to find a guide some place soon. Within a half mile of the house, they came upon a wide deep swamp. In order to cross over, the men were forced to strip naked. Because of the rough terrain, they only traveled about five miles that day. At evening they came to three Indian cabins. "They are called black houses since they have no windows," one of the men said. "I've been here before. This is where my father-in-law lives."

"I didn't know you were married," Lawson said.

"They think I am. The old man gave me his lovely young daughter for my bed. She baked my bread and was my wife while I tarried there."

"So that's what being married is." One of the men poked the horny one.

When they arrived at the house, nobody was home, so the son went to the granary for corn and other provisions to prepare themselves a meal. Before they had been there an hour, they were covered with fleas. "I've seen fleas before," Lawson said, as he swatted and scratched, "but this is worse than a dog kennel."

The old man came in and seemed glad to see his son-in-law.

"My father-in-law is a great conjurer and story teller," the son said. As they gathered around the campfire and passed the pipe, the old man told this tale:

"My people, the Santees were gone to war against the Hooks and Backhooks Nations, leaving the old people and children at home. Many moons passed with no word of the fate of their loved ones. They pleaded with me to find out the condition and location of their fighting men.

"I dressed in a clean white dress made of deer skin. A great fire was built, and the Indians sat around it. I was blindfolded. I walked around the fire three times, then I went into the woods. I returned in about a half hour and surrounded the fire as before, then left a second time to go to the woods. When I returned, a great swarm of flies accompanied me and flew around the fire several times before falling into it.

"I was confused and weak. A huge fire spewed from my mouth, my tongue out while I howled frightfully. An Indian man assisted me back to the fire, where I broke out in a sweat, as wet as if I had fallen in the river.

"After a time I recovered my strength and told the waiting people. 'Your men are near a river which is flooded so they cannot pass over it for several days. Then they will return safely to your fires.'

"And it came to pass as I had said."

The old man invited them to stay the night in his house and take whatever hospitality his cabin afforded. Then he left to go hunting in the woods, perhaps to escape the fleas. But one of the Indians with Lawson said, "The fleas don't bother him. The bear oil protects him."

Since Lawson and his men didn't want to rub the smelly bear oil all over their bodies, they camped out in the woods that night.

FLAT HEADS

As they walked along, one of Lawson's company lingered far behind, incapable of keeping up with the rest. They hadn't realized he was missing until he was out of sight. "Shall we wait here for him?" the second-in-command asked.

"No, let's proceed on our way. We can leave markings to show him the way." Lawson believed the laggard would catch up with them by the time they halted for the night, but when they reached their destination, the man was not to be seen.

On the west bank of the Wateree River [below Camden, South Carolina], they came upon a nation of tall persons, the Wateree Chickanee Indians. "They will steal anything available, in fact they are so adept at it, I believe they would steal with their feet," Lawson wrote.

They were mostly poor, had few English advantages. Several still relied on bows and arrows. Lawson calls them "lazy, a quality incident to most Indians, but none quite so proficient at it as these."

The next morning as Lawson and his men were

shaving, the Indians watched them, obviously coveting their razors. "This is a new thing. Let us borrow your tool that we may try it," one begged.

The day before, they had borrowed his knives, scissors, and tobacco tongs, which were not returned. "This is a magic tool, not to be used by just anybody," Lawson assured them. When he was finished, he hid his razor where it could not be easily found.

As they debated whether they should send out a party to search for the missing man, the laggard overtook them with a Waxsaw Indian as his guide.

"What happened to you?" Lawson inquired.

"I missed the path and came upon another nation of Indians. They entertained me generously and sent me to invite you to visit them. Their feelings were hurt that you didn't take up quarters with them originally."

"These Wateree Indians are of the poorer sort, not capable of entertaining you as you deserve," the guide said.

Bidding the Wateree Indians adieu, Lawson and his party, accompanied by their Indian guide, set off towards the camp of the Waxsaws, where they were welcomed with great ceremony. Furs and deerskins covered cane benches prepared for them to sit on. They were served immediately with stewed peaches and green corn.

These Indians were extraordinary in appearance, called flatheads by their neighbors. In their infancy, their nurses lay the back part of the child's head flat on a board, with a bag of sand on the children's forehead. He was swaddled down hard upon the board from one end to the other, thus making the child's body and limbs straight as an arrow. This caused the child's eyes to look strange when they were grown.

"Why do you do this to your children?" Lawson hesitated, not wanting to insult his host, yet curious.

"It is done to make the eyes strong so we can see deer at a greater distance. The best hunter gets the prettiest of the women." That made sense.

SUGAREE INDIANS

A member of Lawson's party complained of an infected leg. The landlord where they were staying, [near York County, South Carolina] offered to aid the ailing man. He examined it throughly, then he drew out an instrument which resembled a comb, made of a split reed with 15 teeth of rattlesnakes. He bathed the infected leg with warm water spit from his mouth. Then he used the instrument to scratch the place where the lameness lay, until it bled. Then he washed it again in the same manner. After he had dried the infected leg, he scraped off the rind of a sassafras root and beat it between two stones into a powder. This was applied as a poultice, then bandaged.

In two days the patient was well enough to proceed on their journey. They arrived at a settlement belonging to the Sugaree Indians. At the king's house, they met trader John Stewart, a Scot whose home was at James River in Virginia. "May I accompany you on your journey? I have heard it is unsafe for one man alone to travel in this area because of the the warring Sinnagers [Canadian Indians]."

Stewart had heard Lawson was coming and had waited so he could travel with him. Lawson couldn't understand how messages could fly so rapidly from one place to another.

Stewart had brought seven horses, loaded with

English goods to trade with the Indians. "Since I have but little cargo remaining, if you can wait two more days for me to get rid of these goods, I will travel with you."

Lawson, who was in no hurry to proceed, consulted his company, who agreed. They spent the next day preparing to continue their journey. Their landlord, King of the Kadapau Indians, always kept two or three trading girls in his cabin. He offered them to Lawson and his men. Lawson, without allowing his horny young friend to speak, refused for them all.

This caused his majesty to fly into a violent rage, to be thus slighted. He told the Englishmen, "You are worthless, good for nothing. I offer you my hospitality, and you refuse!"

Lawson's horny young man hung his head in embarrassment, having too lately been made a loser by that sort of merchandise. John Stewart and Lawson prepared to depart immediately.

At the next town, an elderly Indian said, "The English have a village they call Charles Town. It is located in the middle of several small Indian tribes of Siouan and Muskhogean. It is good, and it is bad. It keeps the Spaniards and French from coming and taking us away as slaves. But they expect us to furnish them with food."

Lawson wrote in his journal, "The greatest cause of resentment was the fact that the whites made slaves of many Indians. Some of these were sent to the port of Charles Town on Ashley River to be sold or shipped overseas. The name of Ashley River fills Indians with fear. Then too, we white traders daily cheat them in everything we sell. We esteem it a gift of Christianity not to sell to them as cheaply as we do to the Christians." Apparently Lawson saw nothing un-Christian with this practice.

TRADING DIRECTLY WITH ENGLAND

A tribe of Seewes lived near Winyah Bay. "Englishmen are cheating us in their trading. Our skins and pelts are worth more than they are paying us." The Indian who spoke was tall, well-formed, and crafty.

The other men agreed with him. "For our furs all they give us are a few worthless beads and ornaments. Then they take our furs back to England where they sell them for far more."

"How can we circumvent these worthless traders and keep these profits ourselves?" a young brave inquired. "Surely those who reside in England are of a better sort than those thieves who trade here among us."

"If we could take our skins and furs directly to England, we would obtain 20 times as much more from the honest Englishmen," the chief suggested.

They considered the matter for awhile, watched what the traders did, where they came from, and where they went when they left the village. It soon became apparent that the English left in their ships from a certain place and returned to the same site.

"England cannot be far from that place. Surely we are as wise as the white men. Why cannot we build our own boats and sail to England with our merchandise?" the chief asked.

They discussed the matter at length and decided to proceed with this idea. Those who were the best boat-builders were assigned to build more canoes, better and bigger than the usual ones. Others were sent to hunt. Each person was assigned to do what he did best.

"Let this be our secret, do not tell anyone, lest the English should learn of our plans. Do not even tell the neighboring tribes lest they try to copy our plans, thus lowering the value of our barter in England." When the chief spoke, it was taken as an order.

Preparations for the grand journey began. Soon they acquired many furs and a small navy. Provisions, merchandise, and hands were placed aboard, leaving only the very old and very young to remain at home until their successful return.

Since the wind was rising, they set up their mat-sails. However, they were hardly out of sight, when a storm arose and swamped their canoes. Many were drowned, thus entering the "other world." Others were rescued and taken aboard an English ship to be sold as slaves in the Caribbean.

Those few of the Seewees who survived, sit around their bonfires relating again and again the story of their ill-advised, abortive attempted voyage to England.

SWEATING HOUSES

Lawson asked of a certain tribe, "Do you ever get any bezor stone?"

"I am not familiar with this word."

So Lawson described it to them and asked if they knew where it could be found.

"We have plenty of it. What use do you have for it?"

"White men use it for a physic. If you can find some, when I come this way again, I will buy it from you."

Thereupon the Indian pulled out a leather pouch which contained some of the powder. "I am a great hunter. This powder blown into the eyes, strengthens the sight and brain exceedingly."

So Lawson traded two or three flints and a large peach loaf for the powder in the pouch.

Near the town were several sweating houses, made of stone, shaped like a large oven. The Indians used them for the relief of pains in the joints caught by cold or by traveling.

That night the most violent northwest wind he had ever seen, blew down the stockade posts that guarded the town. Lawson was afraid he too would be blown into the river.

The one-eyed king, who was a conjurer, went out into the storm. He used his conjuring power to calm the wind and seas.

"What caused such a great wind?" Lawson asked.

"The Devil was angry because we did not put the Sinnagers to death."

At another house where Lawson and his fellow travelers stayed, they were provided a dish in great fashion among the Indians. As Lawson wrote, "Two young fawns taken out of the does' bellies, and boiled in the same slimy bags nature had placed them in, with one of the country hares stewed with the guts in her belly, and her skin and hair left on."

One of the party objected, "You'll never catch me eating such slop."

That's strange, Lawson thought, he thinks nothing of eating alligator.

They came upon an Indian who was crippled."What happened to that man's feet?" Lawson asked.

"He was a prisoner of the Sinnagers. When he tried to escape, they caught him and cut his toes and half his feet away. Then they lapped the skin over the wound so it would heal. Now he can no longer run. And even if he did, the impression of his half-feet would leave distinctive tracks." Now he remained near his home [Hillsboro, North Carolina].

When they were near one of the Cape Fear tributaries, Indians brought them two cocks, and pulled their large feathers off, singeing the lesser ones. Saying nothing, Lawson took one of the cocks and began pulling the guts out to clean it. Lawson knew the Indians cooked fowl with the innards left in, but he and his men preferred them gutted. He placed the cock in a basin of water to wash it. To his surprise, it wriggled out of his hands. It was alive.

The Indians laughed. "The cock was meant as an offering to one of our gods."

Lawson continued cleaning the cock. They had chicken for supper.

Around the campfire that night, Lawson asked, "Have you had any problem with the whites hereabouts?"

An elderly man began this story:

"Many moons ago, a group of whites came here and

offered us trinkets for land. Of course we accepted. Indians know no one can own land. It is ours to use while we are here, but we cannot own it. A few white people came and cleared land and began planting fields. Our People didn't like them moving into our territory. When we burned the fields to chase out the deer, the settlers attacked. But they were so few and so scattered, we took many scalps. Those who lived left to go back where they came from. They left in such a hurry, they left their cattle and hogs behind. They nailed a note to a tree which some say was a warning for whites to stay away."

"Did they stay away or come back?" Lawson asked.

"More whites came. They scattered all along the river. They took away our children, promising to teach them to read and write and study their Bible. But our children were not returned to us,.the whites made slaves of them. The people attacked. Because of the white man's guns, they seemed to have won, but we continued to harass them until they too moved away."

LAWSON AND LIGHTENING

At one time, the Tuscarora covered most of the land from Virginia almost to South Carolina and from the Piedmont to the coast. When Lawson visited some Tuscarora Indians, late in the afternoon, a little black cloud appeared in the northwest. It increased and spread across the village. Then came the wind and rain and lightening.

So Lawson left the place where they had been feasting and ran down to where his boat was anchored. He covered himself with a blanket to keep out the rain. Lightening came down in long streaks. Lawson was so frightened he was afraid to even breathe. If that lightening had hit a barrel of gun powder in his boat, it would have blown him to pieces.

His fervent prayers were answered, and he was not harmed. But the violent wind had blown the water away. His boat was now rested on dry land.

Then he saw Indian women coming towards him carrying torches. "One of our men was struck by lightening and he is dead," one woman said. Lawson decided to remain to see the internment the next day. When the men cut reeds to make a coffin, Lawson pitched in to help. "See--he is our friend," they said, as they slapped him on the shoulders.

When all was prepared, the Doctor or Conjurer made a speech:

"Lightening comes down from the gods. It will kill everything on earth. It often reaches the porpoises and other fish and destroys them. Everything runs to shun it except for the mice in the corn fields who are too busy eating when it strikes at its worst to heed it."

He added, "No wood tree can withstand it, except the black gum. The lightening will run around that tree a great many times, trying to enter in, but can never accomplish it."

"You must understand that sort of gum tree will not split or rive, therefore I suppose the story might rise from this fact," Lawson said. "Then the doctor began to tell me the most ridiculous absurd parcel of lies about lightening I have ever heard."

He added, "An Indian of our nation once caught lightening in the likeness of a partridge. After that no other lightening could harm him. He kept it for several years, but finally it got away from him. It was a shame, because then he was as liable to be struck with lightening as any other person."

There was an Indian who had lived chiefly in an English house, so Lawson called to him and told him about the lies the doctor had told.

"You are much mistaken, it was not a lie. That old man is almost 100 years old. I know him well. He never did tell a lie. If he said it is so, then it must be true."

Lawson kept his own council.

Then he was told about a Negro someone had killed, then burned his house. The plantation owner complained to the authorities. "It was an Indian. My overseer saw him fleeing the property. I demand he be brought to justice."

The plantation owner, accompanied by the law, went to the Indian king, a Tuscarora. "One of your men killed this man's slave. He demands justice. Search out the guilty party and turn him over to us."

The Tuscarora promised satisfaction. Lawson thought--oh, yeah.

The next day, a young brave was reluctantly presented by the three kings to the white men. "He is the guilty party." After a speedy trial, the young man, trembling in fear, was brought out to be hanged. He accepted his sentence without fighting, a brave man to the end.

"If it had been left to the Indians, he would have suffered much more," Lawson wrote.

The young brave was hanged on a tree near the place where the murder had taken place. The Greats of his tribe attended. They took him by the hand and one of them said, "Thou wilt never play any more rogue tricks in this world. Whither are thou gone to shew thy tricks now?"

Lawson says this shows what kind of men these people these savages really are. "They will save their own men if they can, but if the safety of all the people lies at stake, they will deliver up the guilty. After it is over, they will never pity or think of them more."

SNEAKY WARRIORS-SAND BANKS

On the North Carolina Outer Banks, Lawson was told about two Indian nations who were at war. Each had sent red painted sticks around to other friendly towns inviting them to join in the conflict. The warriors had painted themselves red and black and had parties of men hiding in the woods trying to capture their enemies.

The ones with the lesser number found that a spy had reported their presence. This presented a problem for the smaller tribe.

"We can't go ahead because of the river. They will see us and attack us and we will be killed. We cannot go backwards, the enemy lies in that direction."

They called a Council meeting to discuss the matter, weighing their present circumstances. They debated and argued. Since they were so far out-numbered they could see no way to avoid defeat. This would mean many of them would be killed, and others taken prisoner.

At last a wise old chief suggested a plan which they adopted, "Build a fire like we plan to spend the night in the woods. Before it is lighted, bring logs of wood to the place and dress them in our clothes, so they will look exactly like Indians. Then light the fire. Our enemies will see the logs dressed like men lying by the great fire. Supposing we are at rest, they will come upon us and fire upon us. When their guns are out of ammunition, then we, who have been hiding naked in the valley, will come upon them and defeat them."

They agreed that this was a sound idea. It was done as

the old chief suggested. Towards dawn, the enemy, supposing them to be asleep, fired upon them. Then when their guns were empty, the hidden Indians fell upon them, taking every man among them prisoner to be sold to the English.

Another instance happened between the mainland Machapunga Indians and the Coree Indians who lived on the Sand Banks. Some believe these were Manteo's tribe who lived on Harker's Island and included a remnant of Sir Walter Raleigh's so-called "Lost Colony."

Lawson wrote, "Several of their ancestors were white who could talk in a book as do the English. Gray eyes are found among them and no other tribes."

The Machapunga and Coree Indians had been at war for some time, but had recently concluded a peace agreement. The Machapunga Indians were invited to the Sand Banks for a feast to celebrate their peace treaty. The Machapunga King was stout and a great politician.

The King ordered, "Every man carry your tomahawk or hatchet under your match coat. When I give the signal, fall upon them and slay them."

So it was done.

They set out for the Coree town. The Corees had prepared a great feast of vegetables and fruits and meat and fish for them. They welcomed their guests with love, happy to see the enmity ended.

After the feast was over, they started dancing as was their custom.

The Machapunga king saw this as his best opportunity. He gave the word. The Indians pulled their weapons from under their match coats and attacked their hosts. Several were killed, and most of the remainder were taken prisoner. Only four or five escaped. Several were off in the woods and thus safe.

The prisoners were sold as slaves to the English. At this time neither side had guns. All they had were their bows and arrows and tomahawks.

THE RUM TRADE

Lawson decried the practice of providing rum to the Indians. He said it caused them to commit deeds of violence they would not have committed if not for the strong drink. The English traded it to them for skins, furs, slaves, and other commodities. Once an Indian took a drink, he could not stop until it was gone. An Indian would sell all he had in the world to obtain a drink. Sometimes when drunk, they fell into the fire, fought, or even committed murder.

When Robert Daniel was Governor (1716-17), at the request of the Indian kings and rulers, he met with them and the Government Council to discuss the matter. The Indian rulers wanted a law passed forbidding the English from selling rum to the Indians. The law was passed, demanding a stiff monetary penalty for those who disobeyed it. The rule was never strictly enforced. In fact, some of the young Indians were so disgusted with the rule, they vowed to kill those who had passed it.

Lawson said that the Tuscarora carried on an extensive rum-trade with the inland tribes. The traders brought the rum in rundlets several hundred miles, but sometimes they couldn't resist from breaking open their cargo. They sat and drank it all, getting uproariously drunk.

Other times, they drank only a portion, then filled the container the rest of the way up with water. Those who buy the rum had only one measure--the mouth of the seller, so they chose to buy from the one with the widest mouth. The buyer brought a bowl to put his rum in. If the one who measured it, swallowed some, this often caused fights.

HUNTING QUARTERS

Will, who was acting as guide, took off to search for his lost horse. When he returned, he found two Indians attempting to converse with Lawson, who couldn't understand them. Since Will had been in this area before, he translated, "They say the English are a very wicked people because they threatened the Indians for hunting near their plantations."

Lawson denied any knowledge of this practice. "We wish to trade with you. We will treat you fairly."

The Indians carried wooden bowls and ladles. "We trade with the Schoccores and Achonechies for raw hides. We trade with you. You no trade with the westward Indians. Must trade through us."

In order to frighten the white men, the Indians told such fierce stories that one Indian man and his son refused to accompany them further. Lawson told them, "Do not be frightened. They stole the white man's hogs, that is why the white men are their enemies, for revenge and for restitution."

The next morning, they arrived at Hunting Quarters, the area from Oyster Creek east to Pamlico Sound [now Atlantic and Sea Level]. It was located on the edge of a vast tract of hundreds of acres of hunting grounds of the Indians in the northeast section of Carteret County [North Carolina].

There the English met with about 500 Tuscarora. Their village was laid out with streets. The houses were built with pine bark, but ridge-poled at the top instead of round. Lawson managed to obtain some corn from them, but they refused to sell any game. "No game for trade. Game is scarce. Need to feed our families."

"They are expert hunters," Lawson explained to his men. "The problem is there are too many people for the range." This was true, but it was also true that the white men had begun encroaching upon the Indian lands.

Since this land was near the sea, they harvested fish, clams, and oysters from the waters.

Lawson commented that this was the only time he ever saw a hump-backed Indian.

They came to another Indian town about two o'clock. It was empty except for a couple of old women, the others having gone to Hunting Quarters. No provisions were offered at that place.

One of the Tuscarora who traveled with them, took them to his place in the Lower Quarter where they were fed. Soon they were off on their way towards the Forks of the Neuse.

FORKS OF THE NEUSE

Lawson's party passed through several swamps, not traveling over 12 miles that day. Finally they arrived at a cabin, where the master welcomed them. "If you will tarry with us two days, I will guide you to the company of Indians who trade with the English," he promised.

So they decided to remain. While they were there, a woman had fits. An Indian doctor was sent for. He laid the patient on her belly, then he made a small incision with rattle-snake-teeth. Putting his mouth to the place, he sucked out nearly a quart of black blood and serum. This was supposed to cure her of the fits.

Their landlord presented them with the tail of a beaver. "Very choice food," he said, "and craw-fish, large and tasteful as can be found anywhere."

"Do you find any sturgeon in these waters?" Lawson asked his host.

"Hundreds of them. In the summer time, they often sleep on the surface of the water. Once this spring, one of them was sleeping and floated down the creek, still asleep. One of our Indians ran down the creek ahead of the fish, waiting for the stream to bring the fish to him. As soon as it came within reach, he threw his lasso over the fish's head. This woke the sturgeon, who immediately began thrashing about and dove under the water, dragging the Indian after him. It was a point of honor for the Indian not to let go, so he was almost drowned. Sometimes both the Indian and the fish were seen bobbing up out of the water, then diving down into the deep water again. Finally the Indian managed to suffocate his adversary and hauled its body ashore in triumph."

The Indians along the coast refused to eat sturgeon taken from salt water and would let them rot on the shore, but those taken from fresh water were huge and added to their food supply.

One Saturday morning, their landlord took off with them in search of the English. That afternoon they ferried across the Chattookau River [the northwest branch of the Neuse River] in a canoe. The area was filled with swamps.

Some Indians invited them to their cabins, but they received nothing for their labor except 12 miles of extra walking.

There were many Indian towns and plantations in this area, but they marched all day without finding any provisions. About ten o'clock that night they met an Indian who had a load of shad fish ready to be barbecued. Lawson traded a dressed doe skin for 24 of them.

They traveled on through the swamps. That day, for the first time in over 600 miles, they observed Spanish moss hanging on the trees. In the afternoon, they came to the banks of the Pamlico, about 20 miles from the English plantations by water, but not so far by land.

Their Indian guide revealed a canoe which he had hidden and took them across the Pamlico. They went about six miles farther. That night they laid under two or three pieces of bark, at the foot of a large oak tree. During the night, it snowed and rained with much thunder and lightening.

The next day they traveled about 12 miles to reach Richard Smith's plantation. Hannah Smith, who co-habited with Lawson at his house in Bath, is believed to have been Richard's daughter.

Lawson and Smith agreed that the Indians seldom

stole from each other, but saw nothing wrong with stealing from the whites. The whites saw nothing wrong with taking anything the Indians owned with or without permission. Smith said, "When the Indians hunt in the woods, they burn the woods and sometimes the fire spreads to the white plantations. This is their way."

They agreed that the Indians had become so dependent upon the white man's goods, in a sense, they were enslaved by the whites even before they were captured and made slaves.

Captives were sometimes tortured in indescribable ways. The method was left up to the women to make up for their grief for the men they had lost. It was this which gave the Indians such a reputation as brutal savages.

When the North Carolina government refused to grant the Tuscarora a certificate of good conduct which would allow them to move to Pennsylvania, they had come to the end of their patience. They decided to make war upon the hated colonists.

JOURNEY INTO INDIAN TERRITORY

Baron de Graffenried had declared himself governor of New Bern. As he and Lawson strolled down Front Street in New Bern, Lawson asked,"How would you like to accompany me on a boat trip up the Neuse?"

"Why would I want to do that?" de Graffenried puffed as he attempted to keep up with the quick-footed Lawson.

"Well, we could refresh ourselves by picking grapes along the way. I know because I've been there before. The grapes should be plump and plentiful about now."

"It would take more than wild grapes to make me go

into that savage country." De Graffenried paused, straightening his wig which had gone askew.

"Maybe we could discover what the land is like further up there, and we could see how far upriver we could go."

De Graffenried was not to be persuaded. They parted, each going his own way.

A few days later, Lawson once again accosted de Graffenried. "I've often wondered if we could find a shorter, easier route upriver to Virginia. Then too, I'd like to find out how close we are to the mountains." Lawson knew the possibility of easier trade would tempt de Graffenried. If he wanted to make the trip, he could have gone without the Governor, but he thought it would be amusing to see how the oh-so-proper Governor would react to being thrust into the midst of savages away from the protection of the town. Although de Graffenried had dealt with the Indians close to the settlement, he had never traveled into the savage country.

"That is what you said about New Bern, but it wasn't so. I'll agree to accompany you if we take an interpreter with us. And this time I hope you are telling me the truth, not like last time. Not like when you said you had paid the Indians for the land at New Bern."

Lawson refused to argue about New Bern. They took provisions for 15 days with two Negroes to row the boat and two more as guides. At the last minute, Lawson sent one of the Indians on ahead by horseback to explore the lay of the land. De Graffenried objected, but Lawson ignored his protest.

It was a fine day, the sun was bright in the cloudless sky. It hadn't rained for days, and none was expected any time soon. Fall had come early, so the leaves were turning a glorious gold and russet and scarlet. Due to lack of rain, the river was low, and travel rapid. That night they pulled over to the shore and pitched their tents under the shelter of live oak trees near the water.

Early the next morning, they broke camp to start another leg of their journey.

Meanwhile, the Indian Lawson had sent on ahead on horseback ran into difficulty. When he arrived at a river he had to cross, he came upon the town of Catechna. Whether it was accidental or on purpose, no one knows.

Guards stopped him as he rode in, "Why you ride white man's horse?" The Indians along the coast seldom rode horses.

"I'm on a mission for the Governor." His chest puffed like a pigeon's with pride. "He's with a party going upriver, so I am delivering his horse to him."

This alarmed the Indians. The men of Catechna joined together in a huddle--were the whites planning further intrusion into Indian lands? They took the Governor's horse. Things looked bad for the Indian.

After a conference, he was told, "Your Governor is not to advance any further into this country. Our King forbids it. Tell your Governor he must turn back."

So Lawson's Indian fired his gun into the air, a pre-arranged signal warning Lawson and de Graffenried of trouble.

Lawson heard the signal and acknowledged it by firing his own gun in reply. Since it was already late in the day, they pulled over at the next spring, where they planned to spend the night.

As they were transferring supplies they would need for the night, from the boat to the camp site, the bushes parted, and an Indian appeared. The governor dropped the bed roll he was toting. He reached down and picked it up. "We must return down the river immediately. I don't like that Indian's appearance."

"He appears ordinary to me." Lawson laughed at de Graffenried's discomfort, but since de Graffenried was already on his way back to the boat, Lawson followed.

Suddenly the lone Indian was accompanied by others. They came from the bushes, dropped from trees, and even swam across the river. They swarmed over the white men so rapidly they were unable to defend themselves.

"We're going to be killed, I told you we shouldn't have come," de Graffenried whined.

Even Lawson was becoming edgy. The Indians made them prisoner, took their arms and provisions, and led them away. "Please allow us to remain here overnight," de Graffenried begged. "When dawn comes, we'll proceed down river to see the King of Catechna where we may justify ourselves."

But the Indians refused. If they had been allowed to remain in that place, they could not have traveled far by foot. "No, you come with us."

They were forced to run all night through brambles and shrubs across thickets and swamps. Lawson was in better condition than the more sedentary Governor, who stumbled and fell, complaining all the while.

It seemed the trip would never end, but at about three o'clock in the morning, they arrived at Catechna, King Hancock's town.

Later that morning, they were brought before the king to answer for their conduct. Although Indians usually sat upon the ground, King Hancock sat in regal state with his

Council on a kind of scaffold. The captain who had captured the white men made a long, exaggerated report. Finally the King stood up, and accompanied by his Council, approached the captives.

He spoke civilly, but they only understood a few words.

Then the King left them by the fire, guarded by seven or eight Indians. At ten o'clock, Indians erupted from their homes and clustered together in groups to discuss what should be done with the prisoners. It was decided that since they had not yet had the opportunity to defend themselves, they should not be bound.

At noon, the King served them a kind of bread made out of buck-wheat called dumplin's and some venison in a disgusting dirty fur cap. Since the men were hungry, they ate, then they were allowed to walk through the village.

Towards evening, a great assembly of people from neighboring towns met to discuss how they should avenge themselves for the rough dealings of the wicked English Carolinians who lived near the Pamlico, Neuse, and Trent Rivers. Then too, they wanted to learn what help they could expect from their Indian neighbors.

The matter of the prisoners was brought before the Council. The king ordered the youngest man present to represent the Council. The king asked the questions. The problems were to be discussed first, then a conclusion reached.

"To what purpose have you undertaken this journey?" the King inquired.

"We came upriver for our recreation and to gather grapes. Also we wished to see whether the river is fit for navigation so that we may transport goods by water to trade.

The present route is inconvenient." Lawson spoke slowly, enunciating each word, hoping to make himself understood.

"Why did you not acquaint me with your plans?"

There was no way he could answer this question. Then the King complained about the general abuse his people had endured at the hands of the English inhabitants of the Pamlico, Neuse, and Trent Rivers. Then he became more personal. "You, Mr. Surveyor-General Lawson, have been too severe with my people."

He added, "You sold our land."

"Sir, I have traveled throughout the Indian territories without any problems with any of the tribes. I have dealt fairly with them. I have bought land for myself and arranged for the sale of land to the governor. Your accusation is completely unjustified."

The king continued as if Lawson had not spoken, "Furthermore, your Mr. Hancock took a gun from an Indian and Mr. Price has dealt unfairly with the Indians."

"We are not responsible for their actions, only our own," Lawson retorted.

De Graffenried fidgeted while awaiting their answer.

"It is the decision of this council that you be liberated on the morrow."

The two men each reacted in his own manner. De Graffenried joyfully laughed until he cried, while Lawson sat silent, deep in thought. He couldn't understand why the king had upbraided him for being unfair to his people. He had always attempted to treat them decently even though he knew many of his fellow countrymen didn't. Traveling among them as he had, it would have been suicide not to. Of course what he paid them for provisions and land was not as much as he would have paid white men. What else did they expect?

The following day the two men with their Negroes went down to their boat to prepare for their departure. Some of their belongings had been returned to them, and they needed provisions for the return trip. They both agreed that further travel upriver was both unwarranted and unsafe.

In the meantime, several important Indian leaders, including Cor Tom, arrived to find out more about these two important prisoners. They wished to question them, hoping to learn more about the white man's plans for expansion. They demanded to examine the prisoners themselves. So Lawson and de Graffenried were detained..

The same questions were asked as before. Cor Tom reprimanded Lawson for his actions. "You treated us unfairly. You took our land. In exchange you gave us beads, iron axes, and trinkets, not equal in value for our land."

"I paid you the price you requested. You accepted it."

"Man cannot own land. It is like the water and the sky, placed there for our use, but not to own or destroy."

De Graffenried grabbed Lawson's arm and whispered,. "Don't argue with him. Don't you realize how powerful this man is? He holds our lives in his hands."

Lawson refused to answer him.

After the long examination was concluded, de Graffenried and Lawson were allowed to walk about. "I told you not to irritate him. You should have known better. I'm not ready to die. By your words, you endangered both our lives."

"I have done no wrong," Lawson said.

"You cheated them just like you cheated me. As I told you before, I had to pay three times for my land, once to the Lord Proprietors, once to the Indians, and once to you. You and Cor Tom are two of a kind, pompous asses."

"I've known these Indians far longer then you. I know them best. I know how to deal with savages like Cor Tom." Lawson spat on the ground.

An Indian who understood a smattering of English overheard them arguing and the mention of Cor Tom's name. He reported to the Greats that the prisoners had spoken disrespectfully about Cor Tom.

Suddenly three or four important Indians set upon them, took them by their arms, and led them back to the place where they had been before. This time no mats were spread for them to sit on. Young men grabbed Graffenried's and Lawson's hats and snatched the wigs from their heads and tossed them into the fire. Then some young braves searched their pockets, taking what they had not already stolen and helped themselves to clothes from their luggage.

The Indians called Governor de Graffenried-- Governor Hyde. Hyde was governor of the Colony of North Carolina. One of the Indians corrected him. "This man is King of the Palantines at Chattoocka, not the entire colony."

This should have made a difference, but it didn't. A Council of War was held. At its close, they were sentenced. "Surveyor-General Lawson, you are condemned to die by having your throat slashed with your own razor." This was probably a reference to his refusal to trade his razor to the Indians. "De Graffenried, you too are to die." The method of his death was not specified.

But why were they to die? They had been tried and found innocent. Why the sudden turnabout? They sat all night on the bare ground, trying to digest the sudden change in their fortunes. De Graffenried alternated between reproving Lawson for what he had said and praying for his own soul. Lawson sat stoic as an Indian, closing his ears to the whimpering of his comrade.

At daybreak they were led to the Great Execution Ground. Governor de Graffenried once again attempted to talk to Lawson. "It's all your fault, it was your imprudence that brought us to this unfortunate end. It is best that you make your peace with God." And de Graffenried proceeded to make his own peace with great zeal, much to the amusement of his captors.

But Lawson turned his head away, ignoring de Graffenried, probably wishing that if he had to die, he had chosen a braver companion.

At the Execution Ground, the council had already assembled. De Graffenried's eyes darted around, trying to see if there was anyone who could help him out of his predicament. He saw a savage dressed in white man's clothes. He should know some English.

"Why are we being condemned to die?" de Graffenried asked. "We were to be set free to return to our settlement, why are we to die?"

The Indian ignored him. De Graffenried grabbed his arm. The Indian roughly pushed his hand away. "Why did Lawson quarrel with Cor Tom? And why did you threaten to avenge yourselves on our tribe?"

"It was all Lawson. I am your friend. If you will speak for me to some of the Greats, I will handsomely reward you."

The Indian was obdurate in his silence, but finally de Graffenried thought he had persuaded him. "I am sorry Lawson so imprudently quarreled with Cor Tom. The councilors have seen for themselves how I reproached Mr. Lawson more than once. I am blameless. As to my alleged threatenings, that was a misunderstanding. What happened was that Lawson accused my Negroes in a loud voice for disturbing his sleep during the night. It was only a failure to fully understand English."

The Indian listened to him respectfully but made no comment.

Fifteen minutes later, the Greats came back. Lawson and de Graffenried and the bigger Negro were stripped of their clothes, then their hands and feet were bound. They were forced to sit upon the bare ground, naked, even their heads were bare without their wigs. The big Negro sat behind them. In front of them was a huge fire. Near it stood the conjurer, a grizzled old Indian. Conjurers or high priests were generally magicians, capable of conjuring up the devil. He made two white rounds of either flour or sand in front of the prisoners. A wolf's skin was spread before them. Beside it was an Indian standing in the most dreadful and horrible position to be imagined. He did not move from the spot. He held a knife in one hand and an axe in the other. Apparently he was the executioner.

Displaying great strength of character, Lawson managed not to tremble. He knew the Indians admired bravery in their prisoners. De Graffenried's terror was so immense he was speechless.

Two Indians sat on the ground, beating on small drums, while others sang a mournful tune, almost a wail. Young men, women, and children leaped to their feet and danced with frightful contortions. When there was a pause in the dance, the high priest made threatenings and exorcisms. Guards fired their guns, simulated the dancers, stamping with their feet. When the dance was ended, the braves raced to the woods howling.

Soon they returned, their faces painted in black, red, and white. Some of them had their hair flying, greased all over and sprinkled with minute bits of cotton and small white feathers, and some arrayed in all kinds of furs. They looked like a band of devils as they performed a weird dance around the fire.

Two lines of armed guards stood behind the condemned men, not moving from their post until it was over. Behind them the Council of War sat in a circle, consulting.

Why were they dragging this out? Neither man wanted to die, but the waiting was incredibly distressing. Towards evening, the mob left off dancing to bring more wood from the forest to keep the fires burning all night. A fire in the woods burned so high, de Graffenried thought surely it would consume them all. He knew he was going to die. He prayed loudly all through the long day and night. He remembered his sins, even the least ones. He tried to recall the Holy Scriptures and Psalms and repeated those he knew. He had suffered much, but now he prayed for grace to await his execution with fortitude.

When the sun was nearly set, the council assembled once again. De Graffenried knew that some of them understood English, so he begged, "Can no mercy be shown to the innocent? I have done nothing wrong. It is all a misunderstanding. I did not in any way make threats to any of you. I have always dealt fairly with you. I beg of you to spare me."

When no one appeared to be listening, his voice became stern. "If you do not do so, let me assure you that the great powerful Queen of England will avenge my blood. I am King of the Palantines. It is not proper for a King to be put to death. I brought the German colony to these shores by the Queen's order, not to do you any wrong, but to live in peace with you."

Then he pleaded, "If you will liberate me, I will deliver unto you supplies from the New Bern settlement. And I will serve you in your dealing with your enemies."

Then an Indian who was related to King Taylor, the man from whom he had bought land for the settlement of New Bern, spoke in his behalf. It was decided to send a few members to the Tuscarora village of King Tom Blount, the reigning King of the Northern Tuscarora tribes.

For Lawson, it was another night of anguish and uncertainty. De Graffenried exhorted his Negro to prepare for his death. He tried once again with Lawson. "You must pray for forgiveness for your sins. Before you meet your Maker, you must receive absolution for your sins unless you want to spend eternity in Everlasting Fire."

"You meet your Maker in your own way and I in mine." Lawson evidenced no emotion.

Towards three in the morning, the delegates returned from King Tom Blount with a message concerning their fate. One of the men loosened the cords on de Graffenried. He followed him as a lamb to the slaughter. When they were a few steps away, the Indian whispered gibberish mingled with English in de Graffenied's ear. "You are not to die. Lawson must die."

A crowd of Indians surrounded him, congratulating him, showing much pleasure at his release. His Negro was also released. When de Graffenried attempted to speak to Lawson, he was not allowed to do so.

But Lawson was not forbidden to speak to him. Showing his strength of character to the very end, he said, "Say farewell to my friends in my name."

De Graffenried was led to the cabin of the man who

had spoken for him in front of the council. "Remain here until you receive further orders."

The natives were secretive concerning the method of Lawson's execution. Some said he was hanged. Others said his throat was slit with his own razor.

A letter written by Major Gale, dated November 2, 1711, stated that the Indians "stuck him full of small fine splinters of touchwood, like hog's bristles, and so gradually set him on fire."

So the Indians he had traveled among, admired, and written about, put him to an agonizing death.

LAWSON'S DEATH

In his own book, John Lawson wrote about the cruelty of the Indians towards their prisoners.

"Therefore they inflict on them torment in which they prolong life in that miserable state as long as they can, and never miss skulping of them as they call it."

He goes on to explain what is meant by skulping. He explains how they cut off the skin from the temples and remove it along with the hair, "as if from a night-cap." Then he goes on to describe how they stick pine splinters into bodies and burn the victim alive, the very torture he is believed to have endured.

In Lawson's will, he left everything to his, "Dearly beloved Hannah Smith, the house and lot I now live in, to enjoy the same during her natural life and also one-third part of my personal estate in North Carolina to her proper Use." His daughter and unborn child were to divide the remaining estate.

John Lawson never legally married Hannah Smith.

Other women in the colony were being prosecuted for having bastard children, but no one bothered Hannah Smith, even though Lawson openly lived with her and had at least one child by her.

Marriages were to be performed by a minister or missionary if one was available. If not, then a member of the Council could perform the ritual. Apparently Lawson didn't think it was necessary to officialize his relationship with Hannah. He made Hannah executrix of his will. When he died, he left a "hair trunk" containing some of his writings at the home of William Kirk, who never delivered them to Hannah. [William Kirk appears again in 1718 when he encountered the pirate, Blackbeard].

Lawson had spent months among the Indians, having no problems with them. He knew how to handle them. It is inconceivable that he would have deliberately angered the Greats, as de Graffenried claimed.

The information concerning Lawson's imprisonment and death comes from the writings of de Graffenried. He was supposed to be a colleague and friend of Lawson's, but it is obvious that he was not. Instead of making a plea for clemency for Lawson as he made for himself, he laid all the blame on him. He claimed he was King, so should not be put to death. He blamed the problems about paying for the New Bern land on Lawson. He the same as accused him of land stealing. It is almost as if Graffenried wanted Lawson put to death.

DE GRAFFENRIED RETURNS

The day after Surveyor-General Lawson's execution, the Greats of the village came to Governor de Graffenried. He asked, "What about me? Can I now return to my home?"

The Indian who spoke a little English told him, "We cannot allow you to leave, lest you warn your people of our plans."

"I know nothing of your plans."

"Because of the ill-treatment of your people along the Rivers Pamlico, Neuse, Trent, and Core Sound, we make war upon them. Not until this is over, will you be released."

Governor de Graffenried was shocked. He realized he was in no position to help his people or even to warn them of the coming attack. "But my people at Chattoocka [New Bern] have done you no harm. Cannot they be spared?" If New Bern was destroyed, not only would his life work but all of his belongings would be lost.

The Greats conferred a few minutes. "Your people must go to your town. If they remain in this country, we cannot answer for the evil which may befall them."

De Graffenried was relieved to know they had no plans to destroy his village. Now all he had to do was to find a way to warn his people of the coming disaster. "Is there any among you who will carry a message to New Bern to warn my people?"

Of course there wasn't. De Graffenried would just have to wait and see what happened.

TUSCARORA WAR &
DE GRAFFENRIED

Governor Hyde lived in the more populated Albemarle region in the northeast corner of the colony. Since North Carolina had no permanent capitol at that time, the government met wherever it was convenient for the officials.

ATTACK

About noon on September 22, 1711, an Indian runner burst past the aide into the governor's office. He had run for hours, yet he was not visibly winded. Since Governor Hyde had only recently come from England, he needed a translator. "What's this all about?" he asked his aide, an Indian slave called Matchie.

Matchie was short and squat, a member of the coastal Machapunga tribe. His ability to understand the various dialects made him irreplaceable to the governor. "King Hancock's Tuscarora have attacked the plantations at Bath. At least three houses have been burned, and many people killed."

"When did this happen?" The governor had considered going to Bath that week, but his plans had been unavoidably delayed.

Matchie translated, "Runner says war-whoops woke him early this morning. Mistress and servants were screaming. There were Indians in war paint everywhere. He says he had no weapon except his bow and arrows, so he could not protect them. He slipped out the back way through the woods. The house behind him was on fire. He saw smoke coming from other plantations."

"Does he know what tribe these Indians were?"

"Tuscarora. King Hancock's men. The runner is also Tuscarora, but not of Hancock's tribe."

"Feed this man," he ordered Matchie, "then send runners to the New Bern settlement and to the near plantations to see if this was an isolated incident or more wide-spread."

Matchie did as he was bid. Governor Hyde wasn't unduly disturbed. He was convinced it was only a band of young braves eager to become warriors, but he understood how frightening it must have been for those involved.

But the following day another runner arrived, this time from along the Neuse River. Matchie translated, "Richard Smith sent him. Indians have attacked. Many whites were killed. The woods are full of war-painted Indians, some leading white prisoners."

This was a beastly affair, but what could he do? He was only the governor, a governor without funds. He had no armed militia, and many of his people were Quakers who wouldn't fight. The few men he had, weren't trained to fight against armed ambush. No supplies had been laid aside for such emergencies. He didn't even have the support of many of his people.

Runners arrived from other places, including Core Sound. Tales of atrocities against the citizens were horrifying. "Have the citizens garrison themselves in the tightest houses in each community. Bring the women and children and what supplies they can carry. Collect any available firearms," the governor ordered.

As the governor had decreed, the survivors huddled together in garrisons, leaving their houses and fields open to the savages' fury. The Shackleford plantation on the west side of the North River was fortified. Hammock House in Beaufort sheltered survivors.

The next day word arrived from Roanoke Island and the mainland. "Between 50 and 60 warriors from the Machapunga and Coree tribes attacked and carried off more than 40 whites," Matchie translated.

"But I thought the Machapunga and Coree tribes were at war with one another. How can they be at war one day and unite against the whites the next?"

"It is the way of the People." Matchie was of the Machapunga tribe. Perhaps the governor didn't know.

Messages arrived from other settlements.

Refugees had flooded into Bath from the surrounding area, leaving their fields untended for the Indians to plunder. Governor Hyde was well acquainted with the problems at Bath--summer drought and the yellow fever plagued the citizens. "At least three houses were burned. Lionel Reading's plantation south of the Pamlico has become a fort. The local militia are no help--they are so few in number."

"Why did this have to happen?" Governor Hyde asked again and again of any who would listen.

Finally Matchie hazarded a reply. "The whites cheat at trade."

"But I've been told the Indians abused the fishermen and shipwreck survivors along the coast. Sometimes when they burned the forests while hunting, the fires got out of control and burned crops and houses."

Matchie had dared to speak up when no one else would, but he knew when he had said enough.

Governor Hyde didn't know what he could do. It seemed strange that all of the damage was south of the Albemarle region. This must mean that King Tom Blount, chief of the Northern Tuscarora tribes, was not involved. If he could get him to join with the whites, it would save many lives. But could he trust the man? He was, after all, an Indian. And Indians were not to be trusted.

Governor Hyde made arrangements to meet with King Tom Blount. After the usual amenities, Hyde plunged into his problem. "Are you aware of the attacks upon New Bern and other settlements to the south?" Of course he was aware. Probably he had known about it long before it happened.

The chief admitted this was so. "For weeks the neighboring tribes gathered with King Hancock and planned the war. The Neusick and Coree tribes even moved inland to be closer to King Hancock."

"Are any other tribes involved?"

"The Pamlico, Machapungo, Bay River, and several other small tribes. He has at least 500 men available."

"Why did this happen?" Hyde asked.

King Tom Blount stared at him in disbelief. "You don't know? When the white man came, the People welcomed them and fed them. They offered to share all they had with them, the woods, the sea, the sky. The People believe that no man can own the land. It is here for us to use as is the sea and the sky. We are to leave it as we find it. But the white man wasn't satisfied with this. White man cheated the Indians at trade, took our children off to 'educate' them, then sold them into slavery. More and more white settlers are taking the land where the People have hunted for generations, as it is at Hunting Quarters. Soon there will be no more woods for the Indians to hunt in, no more deer, no more fish. Our women and children will starve."

"We always paid for any land we took." Governor Hyde had been told of the Lawson dispute concerning the sale of the land for New Bern. Hyde couldn't understand the Indians' idea that land couldn't be owned. If it couldn't be owned, what were they getting so upset about?" He had only recently arrived. He knew he was blameless.

"Lawson took the land of the Neusick to establish the settlement of New Bern," Blount accused.

"That land was paid for." This was ridiculous.

"But now Lawson regrets that he cheated us."

"What is that supposed to mean?"

"Lawson and de Graffenried went into Indian country and have not returned."

Had tragedy befallen those leaders? To change the subject, Hyde asked, "Will you unite with us to defeat the Southern tribes?" Hyde didn't know if he could trust him or not, but it was obvious it would take Indians to defeat Indians. Their way of warfare was so different from the white man's. They attacked from behind bushes while the white men fought openly.

"No, no can do. Northern Tuscarora tribes must remain neutral. We refused to assist Hancock's Indians, and we refuse to assist you also. You white men want Indians to fight your war for you. We will not help you, but we will not attack you either." The Northern Tuscarora's economy depended upon trade between North Carolina and Virginia. Of course he wouldn't do anything to destroy this.

So Governor Hyde returned home. He immediately sent a message to New Bern inquiring about the fate of Lawson and de Graffenried. The government had neither funds nor militia. The Lord Proprietors were responsible for the defense of the Colony. They were the owners, but they either couldn't or wouldn't do anything to defend it. He had to obtain help from some place else. So he sent messages to both Virginia and South Carolina, pleading for their assistance.

Governor Spotswood of Virginia sent aid in the form of money and men to stop the Virginia Indians from going south to join the Southern tribes. He persuaded the legislature to appropriate funds and agreed to attempt to gain the assistance or neutrality of King Tom Blount.

A few days later the robbers came back with booty, including several women and children as prisoners. Governor de Graffenried, being careful not to be seen by his captors, spoke to some of prisoners. Some came from Pamlico, others from the Neuse and Trent region. The Indian with whom he was staying, brought home a young boy, the son of one of de Graffenried's tenants.

"Tell me, my boy, what of the others? What of your parents?" he asked.

"The Indian of this house, he be the Devil. He all painted up red and black. He come to our farm. He killed my mother, my father, my brother. He chop them to pieces, all bloody and horrible. I saw it all." He sobbed bitterly.

Governor de Graffenried was not a demonstrative man. The boy's lack of composure embarrassed him, besides if his host believed he was sympathetic with the enemy, he might yet be killed. He recognized some of his clothing and furniture which the Indians had stolen. In a few days, the boy and other prisoners were taken away. He was afraid to ask where they had gone.

The Indians remaining at a camp left the village to

gather wild cherries and dig some yellow potatoes. For the first time, De Graffenried was left alone in the village with no one to guard him. Could he get away? Should he try? If he did, he would have to walk. He didn't know the country which was filled with diverse kinds of dangers, not the least of which were the Indians. If he should come upon even one Indian, he could be killed. They had come to trust him, but if they discovered him attempting to escape, he would surely be tortured and killed.

Besides, they would renege on their promise to save New Bern. As far as he knew, they had not entered the city of New Bern itself, just the out-lying area. After a brief struggle with his conscience, he decided to remain where he was. It was because of his fervent prayers he was still alive-- God would continue to protect him.

Soon the Indians returned to the village for a time of rest. Governor de Graffenried sought out the one who understood English, "When may I return to my people?"

The Indian refused to answer.

"Tell your Greats that we should conclude a private peace. I will provide each of the Greats of your ten villages with a jerkin. I will also provide something more for my ransom-- two bottles of powder, 500 grains of small shot, and two bottles of rum."

"Aw, but the Greats insist on guns and more powder and lead or small shot."

"That I cannot do. It is forbidden under pain of death, to sell or give such goods to the enemy. I wish to remain neutral, to assist neither one side or the other."

Finally the following agreement was decided upon:

(1) Both parties will let bygones be bygones and be

good friends in the future.

(2) The Governor of the German Colony must be absolutely neutral in time of war between the English and the Indians. He will remain in his house and let pass neither the English nor the Indians and do no harm to each. In the event of a misunderstanding they will not avenge themselves.

(3) The Governor promises to remain within his limits and to take no more lands from them without due warning to the King and his nation.

(4) He promises to procure a cessation of hostilities for 15 days so that persons may be selected to propose good and reasonable terms of peace, acceptable to both parties.

(5) The Indians are allowed to hunt wherever they please, unmolested except that they shall not enter our plantations, for fear they should scare away their cattle, and on account of the danger of fire.

(6) Merchandise and provisions have to be sold to the Indians at a reasonable price. No harm will be done to our houses which shall have a special mark on the door.

The agreement was signed by de Graffenried, the Tuscarora Indians, and their neighbors. Due to the intervention of the governor of Virginia, de Graffenried was released. He was on his way home, when the Indians who accompanied him hid him, saying, "Some of the Palatines come."

"How do you know they are Palatines?" If they were really his people, perhaps he could travel the remainder of the way home with them.

The Indians mimicked the Palatines in their gestures, uttering the words, "Ja, ja."

The Indians led de Graffenried through a round-a-about way, across an ugly ditch where they could see a fire afar off. De Graffenried was frightened. He expected he would to be burned to death on that bonfire. To prove the Palatines had not joined with the English, he said, "What you heard were the words 'aye, aye.' This is not German but corrupt English. It means 'yes' in English."

They appeared to accept what he said and continued on their way to where the fire was located. There he found the entire population of the Indian village women and children and those men incapable of fighting.

The next day the neighboring Indians, about 300 armed men, came and gathered together and made war on the 60 or so English and Germans in the woods.

The Palatines, who were not experienced in Indian warfare, were nearly all wounded and one Englishman killed. They had come seeking Lawson and de Graffenried, but seeing they were so out-numbered, they fled back to New Bern. The Indians followed them a short ways, taking horses, victuals, hats, boots from them. De Graffenried recognized his boots in the loot. He knew they were his because they were the only ones made like that, half- boots lined with silver. If they had his boots, it meant the savages had ravaged his settlement. Later he found that this was not so, his people had borrowed some of his things to go on the expedition.

Finally, Governor de Graffenried was allowed to return to New Bern, but he had to walk much of the way.

"When my good people saw me coming from afar, tanned by exposure like an Indian, but on the other hand considered my figure and my blue jerkin, they knew not what to think. In their firm belief I was dead, they thought me an Indian spy, dressed in my jerkin. The men even took up their arms. But when I came nearer, walking with two sticks, and quite lame, they well saw by my look and attitude, I was not an Indian or Savage.

"However, they did not know me at once, but a few came in my direction to raconteur me. When I saw them so puzzled, I began to speak to them from afar, with such a weak voice however, that in their surprise they fell back a few steps, and hallooed to the others to come. I was their lord, whom they thought was dead.

"And so all came in crowds, men women, and children, shouting and crying out, part of them weeping, others struck dumb with surprise. It was a really strange sight, and this medley of sadness and joy, of wailing and delight, moved myself to tears. After having exchanged a few words with those people around me, exhausted as I felt, I at last came home, and after having closed the door of my private room, I made my ardent prayers, giving glory to the Good God for my miraculous and gracious rescue, which may well be held, in these times, for a miracle."

He found the town almost empty. The surviving citizens had gathered at the plantation of William Brice, who had built a fort.

The Indians had respected New Bern's neutrality, but when Brice and his men attacked the Indians, roasting alive the Bay River Indian chief, they retaliated, attacking the New Bern Colony and slew "outlanders and English" alike.

SOUTH CAROLINA COMES TO THE RESCUE

Major Christopher Gale, representing Governor Hyde, was sent to Charles Town to beg for help. The South Carolina Legislature appropriated a large sum of money and agreed to raise an army of friendly Indians to be led by white officers. Colonel Barnwell was placed in charge.

"Why would you expect the South Carolina Indians to come to your rescue when your own Northern Tuscarora tribes won't?" Barnwell asked Gale.

"Financial gain. Any prisoners they take can be brought back to South Carolina to be sold as slaves. Besides we will pay them a bounty for scalps." Indian scalps as well as deer skins had become a form of money for exchange.

The South Carolina army set out to march through 300 miles of wilderness. Along the way, many of the Indians deserted, but others joined. In late January of 1712, when Barnwell arrived at the Neuse River, where they were to be met by Christopher Gale with an army, there was no sign of Christopher Gale or of his army. Colonel Barnwell's army consisted of 30 white men and almost 500 Indians.

But there was no Christopher Gale, nor the army he had promised. A plantation owner told Barnwell, "It wasn't Gales' fault. The North Carolina Legislature refused to supply either men or money for the expedition."

So now what was he to do? He was not familiar with the country, and he lacked a guide. He marched his army on towards the Tuscarora town of Narhantes about 30 miles from New Bern [where Fort Barnwell is today]. The town was well-fortified. On January 30th, Colonel Barnwell attacked. After fierce fighting, his men captured it. Barnwell complained, "While we were putting men to the sword, our

Indians got all the slaves and plunder. We only got one girl."

Later de Graffenried called this town Core Town. It was here he said, "The Indian allies of the North Carolina colonists drove the king and his Indians out. But before this they slew several. They got into such a frenzy over it that they cooked and ate the flesh of one of the Carolina Indians that had been shot down." The attackers were South Carolina Indians and the defenders North Carolina Indians, mainly Coree. [This is the only incident of cannibalism mentioned in North Carolina history].

From there, Barnwell, joined by 67 North Carolinians, marched towards Bath Town on the Pamlico River. On the way they did considerable damage to enemy towns, seizing property and scalps. Some of his Indians stole the acquired loot and deserted. Since the newcomers brought no supplies with them, this further aggravated an already short supply of food.

On March 5th Barnwell attacked Hancock's Fort. He expected an easy victory, instead it turned out to be heartbreaking. The Indians had brought their white captives into the fort. While the battle was ensuing, they tortured the prisoners. Barnwell could hear them pleading for mercy, and it was more than he could bear.

"Release those captives at once!" he roared.

In reply, the Indians sent out an English mother and her five children. "If the attack is not abandoned," she said, "They say they will fight to the death but only after killing the prisoners."

Barnwell consulted with his officers, then he sent back the message, "If some of the prisoners are released immediately, we will meet with the Greats and the remainder of the prisoners at Bachelor's Creek to discuss a peace."

The Indians agreed.

But when Barnwell arrived at the appointed place, the Indians failed to appear with the remainder of the hostages. "Promises, promises--does no one in this God-forsaken land keep their word?" He was becoming more and more irritated with this war.

Barnwell marched on towards Hancock's Fort. A messenger arrived from Governor Hyde. "Food and men are on the way." Another one of their foolish promises. Without waiting for reinforcements, Barnwell attacked the fort. The siege continued for ten days. Failing to take the fort by storm, Barnwell brought up some cannon. This so terrified the Indians they proposed a truce. Barnwell appeared to be near victory, but he accepted a conditional surrender of the enemy. The Indians agreed to turn King Hancock over to him, but Hancock had already fled to Virginia.

"Why did you make peace without my consent?" Governor Hyde asked. "Help was on the way."

"I've heard that promise before. My men were starving. If we had provisions for four more days, we could have made a glorious end to this war."

"Hunger is hardly an excuse for making such a shameful peace when help was on the way," Hyde insisted.

When Barnwell marched into New Bern, he expected honors and rewards for his championship of North Carolina. Instead, de Graffenried and Hyde both ignored him. "No one appreciates what I've done. It almost makes me wish I had let the Indians have it," Barnwell said.

He had promised his men a reward, and he was determined he was not going to send them home without it. Angered, he gathered together a number of friendly North Carolina Indians, captured them, and took them to South

Carolina where they were sold into slavery.

During the summer yellow fever again swept through the colony. Governor Hyde was one of the victims. When they learned of Barnwell's betrayal, this so embittered the Carolina Indians, they no longer trusted white men, and they continued a type of guerrilla warfare.

North Carolina once again called upon South Carolina for aid. Surprisingly enough after what had happened before, they agreed, even though the note insisted that Colonel Barnwell not lead the group. After being treated so shabbily, he probably wouldn't have anyhow.

In March of 1713, Colonel Moore laid siege to the Indian town of Catechna. After three days, the battle was over with a loss of more than 900 Indian lives. The war continued until the fall, when King Tom Blount finally came to the aid of North Carolina. In appreciation, he was named Chief of all North Carolina Tuscarora tribes.

On February 11, 1715, a treaty of peace was signed. Those who refused to follow King Tom Blount were assigned to a reservation at Lake Mattamuskeet in Hyde County.

Eventually the whites decided they wanted this land too. History repeated itself. Some Turcaroras fled and joined other tribes. In 1803, 155 Tuscarora families and seven chiefs left to go to New York, where the chiefs signed away all rights to their North Carolina land.

Later others were gathered up and put on buses and dumped in Robeson County near the Lumbees. Those who refused to go remained as unobtrusively as possible.

Later North Carolina repaid South Carolina by coming to their aid when they had their own Indian problems.

INDIAN CHARITY

While being held prisoner, de Graffenried was stunned by the generosity and pity shown to him by a widow woman who always saw that he had plenty of food to eat.

He was a vain man and tried in whatever circumstances he found himself to remain neat and well-dressed. So he was much disturbed when soon after his capture, the young men took many of his possessions from him, including his sliver shoe buckles.

When the widow woman saw this, she was greatly disturbed. She removed her beautiful brass buckles which were fastened to her head band and tied them on his shoes. Still not satisfied, she searched until she found the one who had taken de Graffenried's buckles. She bought them back from the thief and came running to de Graffenried in great glee.

"Me got'em! Me got'em!" She knelt at his feet and tied the buckles back on his shoes.

De Graffenried stated, "Must it not be concluded that it was a great kindness from a savage woman, for the confusion of many Christians? I must state here, to the shame of the later, that the Indians are generally much more generous and charitable [than the Christians]."

THE BROKEN IDOL

Near the settlement of New Bern, de Graffenried noted a kind of alter, made of interwoven small sticks in a dome-like structure with a small door where the supplicants could place their offerings.

He said, "In the middle of this heathenish chapel was

a concavity where they sacrificed beans, corals, and other articles."

An idol faced east to catch the rising sun. It was carved and its head was painted half red and half white. On the other side of the alter was another idol facing the setting sun. Its face was horrible and painted black and red. The first was obviously a good god and the second one a demon.

One of de Graffenried's tenants, a strapping young fellow, happened to be passing by and stopped to examine the idols. He was infuriated when he saw the second image. It was black and red on a red background. Since New Bern's colors were red and black, he took this to mean that New Bern was a demon.

Enraged at what the young man considered an insult to his town, he took his ax, and with one stroke, split the statue in two pieces.

By the time he had returned home, he had calmed down. "With one stroke I split the devil in two," he bragged.

Soon after this the Indian King came to de Graffenried, complaining loudly about the sacrilege. "One of your men dared to destroy one of our gods. You must locate whoever did this horrible deed and turn him over to us for just punishment."

De Graffenried took it as a big joke. "It was only the wicked idol so no harm was done. If he had cut the good idol to pieces, I would have rigorously chastised him. In the future orders will be given so that no such a thing happens again."

When the King saw that de Graffenried took it as a huge joke, his countenance changed to one of wrath. De Graffenried, seeing that the Indians took what had been done seriously said, "The man's actions did not please me either. If you will show me the one who did this atrocious deed, I will see that he is rigorously punished."

Then to appease the King, de Graffenried treated him and those with him to mugs of rum. When the Indians left, they were in a more serene, quite satisfied, mood.

THE CONJURER

De Graffenried said the Indians had interesting ways to treat the sick. When someone appeared near death, the priest would give whatever remedies he felt were needed. If this didn't work, he made "grimaces, faces, and contortions, blowing at last his breath in the patient's mouth with a loud noise and snoring. If the sick person gets better, the joy is unutterable. If he dies, they howl in a most dismal way," de Graffenried said.

He was present at the death of a widow. At her burial, something peculiar happened. A little flaming fire like a torch or candle light rose from the tomb. Silently it lifted straight up in the air until it passed over the widow's house. From there it flitted across a big swamp until it finally disappeared into the woods.

Governor de Graffenried was so startled at the sight, he asked the Indians who were with him, "What is the meaning of this?"

The Indians laughed, "it is no big thing."

"But what is the meaning of this?" the governor repeated.

"It is a happy omen. She is a happy soul. If the smoke had been black, it would have been an unpropitious sign."

The governor knew the flame could not be artificial. It could have been sulfurous vapors, but it didn't appear to be. Later when de Graffenried was in Governor Hyde's house with the Council and some Indian Greats, he asked an Indian priest, "What was the meaning of the flame rising from the sepulcher at the widow's burial?"

"Only old priests of great experience can cause such visions to appear."

"But what was it?"

"It was the soul of the deceased. It went into another creature. Since she was a good person and well-behaved, it went into the soul of a good creature. However, if she had led an evil life, then her soul would have gone into an ugly, wicked unhappy creature."

Not satisfied, de Graffenried asked, "How does a priest obtain such great power?"

The priest explained, "Sometimes a small, subtle fire, also like a kind of flying flame, flickers from one tree to another. This seldom happens. When an Indian sees it, he must run with all his might to catch it. In the moment when the hand covering the fire extinguishes it, is born a kind of small spider which runs hither and thither very quickly in the hand. It is nearly impossible to keep the other hand closed over it. That way the man who captured this wonderful thing becomes the best master and magician and can achieve all kinds of surprising feats.

"This is how I became a conjurer."

THE GOOD WIND

An old Indian man told Governor de Graffenried this story:

One day a small sail boat was becalmed in the middle of Core Sound. Since they were not expecting to be out on the water for any length of time, they had not carried

128

sufficient provisions. The pilot was anxious, not only were they short of food, but the water was running low. The men were irritable, quarreling over every little thing. Would that they could proceed on their way.

An Indian who was on board, came to the pilot, "If you want me to, I can raise up a good wind for you."

The pilot was pleased. "If you can do so, you will be amply rewarded." But he didn't really think it was possible.

All at once a strong wind arose. A wind so violent, the boat skinned through the suddenly appearing white caps, hitting them like a repeating drum roll. The boat went out of control. The men were so frightened, certain they would be wrecked and drowned, that they grabbed hold of anything they could, even each other.

The pilot couldn't steer. He had lost control over the boat. All he could do was to pray the boat wouldn't crash on shore.

To his great surprise, the boat slowed down and slipped into the space where they had intended to dock. So weak he could barely stand, the pilot climbed from the boat and stood on the sandy beach.

"If my life depended upon it, I would never again seek a strong wind from such a man."

Soon after he returned to New Bern, de Graffenried apparently mortgaged the people's land, embezzled their money, and carried off everything valuable he could find. He promised to return with supplies for the war, but was never heard from again.

WILLIAM BYRD & BEARSKIN

Colonel William Byrd tells about an expedition he took in 1728 to survey the boundary line between North Carolina and Virginia. They began in March at Currituck Inlet.

Since he was unfamiliar with the territory, he planned to pick up guides from the various tribes along the way. One of these was an interesting character, a Saponi named Bearskin. He was hired to act as guide, translator, and hunter.

One night, the other hunters returned toting a fat buck and several turkeys. Bearskin watched the hunters as they prepared the buck and turkeys to stew in the same pot. "No can cook turkey and venison together. Bring much bad luck for future hunting."

"Didn't realize you were so superstitious," one of the hunters laughed.

"Maybe so, but if I shoot turkey and know you cook venison, I hide turkey until next day." Bearskin sat on the ground, a scowl on his face.

Later that night, after the meal was concluded, the men gathered around the campfire. "The good God blessed us greatly in our hunting today," Byrd said, curious to see what Bearskin would have to say about that.

He wasn't disappointed. "There is a Supreme God who made the turkey and the deer for our use. It was he who created the Sun and Moon and Stars. Not only did he create them, he has been keeping them in running order since then."

"Is this the only world your Supreme God has made?" Byrd asked, egging him on.

"Oh, no, he form many worlds before this one. When

these worlds grew old and the inhabitants were dishonest, he destroyed both the inhabitants and the world."

As more white men gathered around the fire, Bearskin continued, "Supreme god is a good god, and he is pleased with those who possess good qualities. Them he places under his sheltering wing. He makes them wondrous rich with plenty to eat, keeps them free from sickness, and protects them from their enemies."

A man from the outskirts of the crowd asked, with a smirk in his voice, "And what of those of us who do not possess your god's good qualities? Those of us who lie and cheat and steal?"

"Telling on yourself?" an old man asked.

Bearskin glared at the one who admitted he was liar and a cheat. "You he punish with sickness, poverty, and hunger. Then you be knocked on the head and scalped by your enemies."

"See--he's talking about you." The old man poked his friend in the ribs.

The man drew back his fist as if to strike the old man, but Byrd intervened, "What about after death?" he asked, bringing Bearskin back to the subject.

"Both good and bad are led by a strong guard into a great road where they travel together for some time. They come to a fork in the road, the way to the right is level, other way is steep and stony and mountainous."

"Which way do the good ones go?" the old man asked, already suspecting the answer.

"A flash of lightening divides them, good go to the right. At this entrance, a venerable old man sits on a richly woven mat. He examines all those brought before him. If they have behaved well, guards open the crystal gate for them to enter into the land of delights. Here it is always spring, the people are young, and the women are bright as stars and never scold."

"Sounds good to me," said one man who had joined the expedition to escape a shrewish wife.

Bearskin went on, "The left road is rugged and uneven, leading to a dark, barren country where it is always winter. At the entrance sits a dreadful old woman on a monstrous toad-stool. Her head is covered with rattlesnakes instead of hair. Her glaring white eyes strike terror into all who behold her. Here the people are always hungry. The women are ugly and have claws like a panther they use to claw men who are slight in passion. These women expect a great deal of love and cherishing. They talk constantly in shrill voices. The ugly old woman pronounces sentence upon those who hold up their hands at her tribunal. They are delivered to huge turkey-buzzards that fly away with them."

The men laughed at the one who had admitted he was evil.

Byrd sat transfixed by Bearskin's story. "Is there no relief for these poor wretches?"

"The god is a good god. After a certain number of years, according to their guilt, they are driven back into this world to be given another chance to mend their evil ways and thus attain heaven."

The white men and the Indians sat quietly contemplating their own lives and probable destinations.

THE YAMASSEE WAR

Soon after the Yamassee Indians returned home from helping North Carolina fight the Tuscarora War, they plotted against the people of South Carolina. On May 23, 1715, Governor Craven wrote a letter to England's Secretary Lord Townsend, informing him of South Carolina's condition and desperate need of assistance.

[The following message is true as told in North Carolina's "Colonial Records." The language has been changed to make it easier to read.]

Honorable:

The neighboring Indians with whom we have had a long continuing amity, has for the past two months been engaged in a most bloody war against this part of your Majesty's possessions. I give you a plain and true account of the present state of the colony.

It is not necessary to acquaint your Lordship with the importance of South Carolina as a buffer colony between the Spaniards at St. Augustine and the French at Mobile. Since St. Augustine is not above 70 leagues from our settlements, it is our belief that the Yamassee have received encouragement from them to make war upon us. The Yamassee are a most warlike nation. With their confederates and allies, we estimate that we have at least 3,000 Indians engaged against us. With all of these until now we have had constant trade and commerce.

About the middle of April, one of the Yamassee Indians gave a hint to a trader or two who lived among them of a design to cut off the English and so become sole masters of their fine and flourishing plantations.

This astonished the poor traders and caused them to beg enough time to come to Charles Town and return. They assured the Indians anything possible would be done to give them satisfaction. The Indians agreed.

The two traders rode all night and day to acquaint me with what happened. The Council was called. We dispatched messengers to let the Indians know some of our chief men would meet them at an appointed place to hear them and redress their complaints and grievances if they had any.

The Indians had waited for the arrival of the messengers. Within 12 hours, the whites had been knocked on the head by the Indians. Several other white people were also barbarously tortured and murdered.

Some of the adjacent settlements were immediately destroyed by the Indians, but most of the people escaped by a wonderful providence. Messengers brought me this horrible story.

I soon mounted a party of men and, accompanied by a small number of Indians, marched and attacked the Yamassees before they could be joined by other Indians. It pleased God to give us victory against a much larger force. Because of their loss, they deserted their towns and settlements, leaving good provisions and plunder for our men. After they escaped, they hid in inaccessible swamps.

The country is now fortifying itself in several places. People are so busy working on defense that all other business has been laid aside, so there is hardly any rice or other crops planted for next year.

There are not more than 1500 white men in the colony--all far apart from each other or in forts, so we need more men for protection. Because of this, I have caused abut 200 stout Negro men to be enlisted. These with a party of white men are marching towards the enemy, but we need arms and ammunition.

I am sending to New England, but I am afraid they cannot sufficiently supply us with our needs. In addition, I am trying to win back some of the Indians on our side by presents or whatever other means possible.

It would be a great pity for such a fine flourishing country as this to be lost because of want of men and arms. This colony is beneficial to the crown by its trade. It also has been of assistance to the other colonies because of the large number of Indian alliances. If we are driven from here, the French from Canada or from old France will certainly get a footing on this land. From here they, joined by other Indians, could march against all or any colony of the main and threaten the whole British settlement.

People are so frightened that many want to leave the colony. It would help to keep them if I could have his most sacred Majesty's assurance he will send them a speedy, sufficient supply of everything.

I am persuaded your Lordship will take the calamities now befallen a distressed people to heart. You will receive everlasting acknowledgments from them and from

Your Lordship's most obedient humble servant,
Charles Craven

Governor Craven's early victory gave South Carolina time to regroup and to prepare for further hostilities. The Yamassees were not alone. They were allied with the Catawbas, Congaree, Creek, and Cherokee. The possibility of 6,000 warriors against them was enough to cause Governor

Craven to plead for help any place he could.

He sent pleas for aid to North Carolina and Virginia, as well as New England and mother England.

Governor Eden, who had recently been appointed governor of North Carolina, called his council together. "Remembering how willingly South Carolina came to our assistance in the recent conflict, how shall we answer Governor Craven's request?"

"We have not sufficient for ourselves," one member said.

"But where would we be today without their aid?" Eden said.

After a heated discussion, it was decided to organize two groups of volunteers. If there weren't enough volunteers, some would be chosen.

Colonel Theophilus Hastings sailed south in the man-of-war "Sussex" with 80 whites and 60 Indians. Colonel Maurice Moore [brother to Colonel James Moore, commander in the Tuscarora War] marched overland by way of Cape Fear with 50 men.

Both Moore and Hastings were originally from South Carolina who had come north in the Tuscarora War and remained.

With this aid and what was sent from Virginia, Governor Carven administered a crushing defeat upon the enemy. The Yamassee were driven from the colony and forced to seek refuge among the Spaniards of Florida.

It was during this war that the English came for the first time in conflict with the Cherokee, well--known for their cunning, war-like tendencies. After the Yamassees were defeated, the Lower Cherokee sent a number of chiefs to Charles Town, "We desire to cease fighting."

Governor Craven decided to send an expedition to their territory to make the peace. The expedition consisted of Moore's North Carolinians and a group of South Carolina men under Colonel George Chicken, with Colonel Maurice Moore in command.

Colonel Moore moved up the north bank of the Savannah River, where he made his headquarters in the middle of Lower Cherokee country.

"What is the reason for these attacks?" Moore asked.

The chief told him, "It is your traders. They have been very abusing of late, but we want peace."

"The white governor will admonish the traders for their actions and forbid them to behave that way in the future," Moore assured them.

The Upper Cherokee refused to parlay. Colonel Moore sent a strong detachment against them by Colonel Chicken. They went into the very heart of Cherokee country near the present town of Murphy in North Carolina.

"What is it you want from us?" Moore asked.

"We wish to go to war with a neighboring tribe. To do this, we need large amounts of guns and ammunition."

"Your petty wars are not our concern."

"They should be. If we make peace with the English and can no longer make war upon them, we will have no place to get slaves to buy guns to make war upon our enemies."

"If the English agree, we will trust them once again."

Finally the English agreed to furnish the Cherokee with 200 guns to make war with tribes the English were still at war with.

After spending the winter with the Cherokee, Colonel Moore returned in the spring of 1716 to Charles Town. He was given a flattering reception. He was invited to speak before the General Assembly to receive thanks from them for so generously coming to their assistance. It was much different from the thanks South Carolina's Colonel Barnwell received after he had rescued the North Carolinians.

OSCEOLA: A GREAT CHIEF

No matter where the Indians lived, if the land was desirable, the whites pushed them off, usually further south. Finally the government undertook a shameful program to move the Creek Indians west. So many sickened and died along the way, it was called the Trail of Tears.

At the end of the Creek Wars, many of the surviving Creek Indians went South to Florida to join with the Muskogee-speaking Seminoles and the Hitichi-speaking Mikasukis. Here they were joined by escaped slaves. The white men lumped them all together and called them Seminoles, Cimmarons, renegades, or runaways.

Osceola, who rose to become a great Seminole battle chief, was born about 1803 along the Talapoosa River near the Alabama-Georgia border. The man he called father was an English trader named Powell. Possibly he was a step-father. It is believed that his mother, Polly Copenger, who had some white blood, was the daughter of a Seminole chief.

While he was still a child, Osceola and his mother moved to Florida. In his teens, he fought in the First Seminole War (1817-18). He was captured along the Enconfino River by General Andrew Jackson's troops, but he was soon released.

The Indian Removal Act of 1830 stated that the Seminole were to be moved west of the Mississippi. Another treaty signed in 1833 by some of the Seminole leaders gave all Indians three years to leave Florida in exchange for land in the west plus money and clothing. It also stated that all Seminoles with Negro blood were to be treated as runaway slaves. Some of them were slaves or children of slaves who had escaped from cruel masters in South Carolina. They ran to the swamps where they joined the Seminoles.

In April of 1835, Indian agent Wiley Thompson, attempted to enforce the terms of the treaty. "Those uppity black Seminoles are an intolerable problem. They own horses, cattle, hogs, and chickens. They live like they were white. They even own guns. They're a danger to us law-abiding white folks."

The Seminoles did not leave during the required three years.

Osceola was not a hereditary chief, he earned his title because of his abilities as hunter and warrior and his stand against deportation. His first wife was a beautiful young woman, a chief's daughter, a combination of white, Negro, and Indian. Since she was part-Negro, in 1835 she was seized as a slave by her mother's owner. She was sold at auction, standing naked on the auction block.

Osceola was furious.

When he was presented with a new treaty he refused to sign it. Instead he slashed the document with his knife and a few choice words. "This is our land. We will not leave. You stole my wife. She was no man's slave. The time will come when you will rue this day." Osceola spoke slowly, enunciating each word. This frightened Thompson more than as if he had shouted.

But Thompson had a job to do. "I am the one with the power," he said. "Place that man in irons."

When his lieutenant objected, Thompson argued, "Osceola repeatedly reviled me. And the language he used would shock a sailor. I have no choice but to have him arrested."

This made sense, but what didn't make sense was placing Osceola in irons for six days. His Seminole pride was insulted. Seminoles like all other peoples, had unruly members, but no Seminole was ever confined or chained for misconduct. Sometimes adulterers were whipped or their noses or ears clipped for their actions. Exclusion from tribal rites and rituals was the accepted punishment for minor crimes. When a murder was committed, the guilty party's fate was decided by many men, usually ending by him being either banished or executed.

But no Seminole, no matter what the offense, was ever chained. He finally signed and was released and escaped into the wilderness where he went from tribe to tribe, exhorting them against complying with the treaty.

To escape the forced removal, the Seminoles began moving their families to the Everglades.

On December 28th, 1835, several days after he was released, Osceola attacked and killed Wiley Thompson, along with an army officer and five civilians. This was the beginning of the Second Seminole War.

Treaty after treaty had been signed and broken by the white men. The Seminoles, once loosely banded, now had a hero, the war chief, Osceola. Under his leadership the Indians learned to work together, to attack, then disappear into the wilderness of their swamps.

"A few companies of regular army men should be able to quell the disturbances caused by a handful of savages," officers told each other.

"We need this land. Reservations in the west should suffice for these savages," the general said.

Many of the Seminoles followed Osceola into the Everglades. They dug in and left only to attack superior numbers with the swiftness of the wind, the silence of the dead. White settlers-- men, women, and children were horribly killed and mutilated.

Osceola hated the idea of killing women and children, but his braves were not so squeamish. Neither were the whites. They destroyed whole villages of Indians, down to the last babe in its mother's belly.

Osceola believed that an Indian who would leave his own people to aid the whites should forfeit his own life, so he led a small war party to Charlie Emathla's farm. Osceola accosted him, "Why you sell your cattle?"

Emathla tried to bluff it out, but he knew he had been caught. "Too many cows." But his eyes shifted towards a money bag lying on the table. "No accept white man's offer of money."

Osceola struck Emathla, "You lie!" And he killed the man. Then in a gesture of contempt, he scattered the coins Emathla had received from the whites on his dead body.

General Jessup and his men stormed Osceola'a headquarters in January of 1837 and captured Osceola'a personal bodyguard, 52 black and three red Seminoles.

They fought on. As the British had already learned, the trained army sent by the United States government was incapable of defeating the Indians in their native warfare.

On December 28, Major Francis Dade and his troops were massacred. Osceola and two or three hundred followers took to the Everglades, where he fought for a year with great energy and skill the superior numbers sent against him.

General Jessup attacked black Seminole villages and held women and children hostage, threatening to sell them to the Creeks as slaves. They were released when the Seminoles said, "Fine. We will capture your women and use them to replace out wives."

Osceola and his men rescued almost 700 Indians

waiting to be sent west.

On October 27, 1837, Osceola went to Fort Augustine to attend another peace parley with the whites. He was wearing a bright blue shirt and red leggings with a red print shawl draped around his head, neck, and shoulders. Osceola was hit in the head. His entire peace envoy, including Wild Cat, were surrounded and captured.

Even some of Jessup's own officers objected to his disgraceful behavior. "What you did was inexcusable," his aide said. "They were under a white flag of truce." Jessup ignored him.

They were imprisoned in a 38' by 18' cell in an old jail while waiting to be transferred to the western reservations. Wild Cat and John Horse began making plans to escape. He told Osceola, "I will be free again or else die in the attempt."

It took weeks to accomplish, but finally they weakened a bar sufficiently to crawl out. One night 20 Seminoles, including two women fled to the swamps where they existed on roots and berries for five days until they reached friends.

Osceola probably could have gone with them, but he realized that he was ill and would only be a determent to the others. Osceola and the remaining prisoners were taken to Fort Moultrie near Charleston, South Carolina.

He was a bitter man. He would rather die than remain prisoner.

Here George Catlin, noted for his Indian portraits, visited Osceola. Cartlin painted Osceola and wrote an account of his death. "Osceola was afflicted with deep melancholy," he said. "He felt that his life was no longer worth living."

Osceola ordered his wife and children to bring him his magnificient battle outfit. After he was dressed in it and wearing his war paint, he lay back down and turned to his wife, "It is finished."

Catlin said, "he grasped his scalping knife in his right hand and calmly died." Catlin's account is unclear as to whether Osceola actually stabbed himself or if he simply died. Some claim he died of abuse or poison by the guards. Others say he died of maleria, January 31, 1838.

Osceola's body was buried on the army base on Sullivan's Island, South Carolina. But Dr. Wheedon, who was Osceola's physician, cut off Osceola's head and preserved it. His descendants say that when the good doctor's children misbehaved, he would hang the head on the bedpost to frighten them. At his death, the head was passed on to his son-in-law, Dr. Daniel Whitehurst, then to Dr. Valentine Mott. It lay in Dr. Mott's museum until it was destroyed by fire in 1866.

Many Indians had been forced West. But others would never leave. Congress passed the armed Occupation Act, allotting huge quantities of Florida land to those who would settle on it. There was no huge battle at the end. No fuss or celebration. The last of the Indians did not surrender. The controversy just sort of peetered away.

SIOUAN TRIBES

Most of the Carolina Indians were distantly affiliated with the Iroquois tribes, but several were Sioux.

The Waccamaw lived in South Carolina, and the Saponi, Keyauwee, Occaneechee, and the Saura were in North Carolina. The Catawba, called the River People, lived in river bottoms along the North-South Carolina border. They referred to themselves as the Real People and spoke a Siouan language.

The Waccamaw, Peedee, Winyaw, and Sewee and other small tribes in the area united in order to survive.

CATAWBA

In order to protect themselves from the fierce Iroquois who came down from the North and their deadly enemies, the Cherokees to the West, the Catawba built their houses within stockades. No one knows why they did it, but instead of taking their garbage outside, they piled it up against the inside wall. The villages stank of decayed garbage.

The Catawba and the Cherokee tribes were sworn enemies and often attacked one another, but the Catawba were usually friendly with the colonists.

When John Lawson visited the various Carolina Indian tribes in 1710, the Catawba were a large, powerful tribe. But soon after his visit, the population declined rapidly. Wherever Lawson went, he carried with him the white man's diseases, especially small-pox. Since the Indians had no natural immunity, many died. Not only did the white men introduce strange illness, they brought strong liquor which killed many.

In 1748, a Catawba warrior named Haiglar became a king. At that time, the line separating North and South Carolina was in dispute. Although the Catawba probably lived in South Carolina, they had problems with both governments. King Haiglar represented the Catawba and acted as a buffer in conflicts.

A meeting was held at Salisbury, North Carolina, August 29, 1754 to discuss the settlers' complaints against the Indians. The Chief Justice spoke first. "As you know, we have met here today to discuss various complaints brought against the Catawbas. We are honored to have King Haiglar with us today to speak for the Indians."

King Haiglar stood tall and proud. He gazed over the audience, which consisted of planters and officials. Some of them he recognized, but others were strangers. "Brothers and Warriors, I am exceeding glad to be able to meet here and talk to you this day. We meet in brotherly love. I am here to answer complaints which have been brought against our people."

Mr. William Morrison leaped to his feet, determined to be the first to protest. He was a portly man and spoke with a lisp. "Certain Indians insulted me at my own house. They came to my mill and threw a pail of water into my meal trough. When I attempted to prevent them, they tried to strike me in the head with their guns."

"It is the custom of our people to throw a handful or two of meal into water to make a drink," King Haiglar answered in a soft voice.

"I could have been killed," Morrison said, his lower lip trembled.

King Haiglar faced his complainant, towering over him. "Mr. Morrison, if you or anybody else had been killed, we would have had to kill the one who did it."

"How can we believe you?" Morrison snorted.

"Recently one of our young fellows, who was on his way to the Waxhaw Settlement, got drunk and killed a little girl. He was immediately seized by our own people. We required another of our young men, a cousin of the guilty one, to kill him. This he did in the presence of some of our brothers."

Then James Armstrong, a planter, charged, "Your men took bread, meat, meal, and clothes from my house. They also attempted to take away a child and threatened to stab those who would oppose them."

"In answer to the charge of taking food," King Haiglar said, "when we go to war, we have no way to obtain food, so we go to the houses of settlers asking for what we need. It is our custom to feed travelers. But when James Bullin and his men came near your house, your dogs warned you they were coming. This gave you the opportunity to hide your provisions. If you act churlish and ungrateful to us, then we must search for food."

"But I gave him food," Mr. Armstrong said.

"You gave him a small cake of bread. Bullin shared this with his men, but they were still hungry. When he asked for more food, you claimed there was no more food in the house. You lied. Whereupon Bullin lifted up a bag which covered more bread. Then one of your women struck him over the head. So of course they took that which they required."

Not giving Armstrong a chance to answer, King Haiglar continued, "You accused us of trying to take a child from among you. It was only done by our young fellows as a way of a joke, expecting the parents to join in the laugh."

"It wasn't funny," Young said. "Your young men stole knives and other things from my house."

"As to our wild young fellows taking knives, clothes, or other such things which do not belong to them, they were drunk."

"That is no excuse," Armstrong said.

For the first time that day, King Haiglar spoke with anger. "You are to blame for this. You rot your grain in tubs and make strong spirits. You sell it to our men. Sometimes you even deliberately give it to them. Then they commit these crimes that you complain about. It is bad for our people. It rots their guts and causes them to get very sick. Many of our people have died lately because of the effects of your strong drink."

Then he pleaded, "Mr. Chief Justice, your honor, I wish you would do something to prevent our young men from doing these things as a result of strong drink."

"We will pass laws regarding this," the Chief Justice promised.

"We do not have strong prisons to place our offending young men in like you do. The only recourse we have is to put them under-ground, which we dislike doing. But we will do it if it is necessary," King Haiglar said.

Then McKnight accused them of stealing his horses and mares.

"A great many of our horses run loose in your lands. And you have stolen many horses and mares from us. Not long ago, we caught a white man with some of our horses and sent him to justice. However, he was not punished for his crime."

"Where did you take him before justice?" the jurist asked.

"Before Mr. McGrit in South Carolina below the Waxhaw settlement."

"Well, no wonder. We have no authority in South Carolina."

"It makes no difference whether the land upon which we live is in North or South Carolina, it is our land. When the Great Man above made us as He did, this color and this hue [he held out his arm to show its color], He fixed it so our people will inherit this land. When the white man came, we attempted to live among you in peace. We had our own way of living, using bows and arrows. We had no knives. We cut our hair by burning it off our heads and bodies with coals of fire. Our axes were made of stone. We dressed in furs.

"But when you white men came, we enjoyed the clothes and the other things you brought. It is our desire to live in love and peace with our neighbors."

"What of the white woman you had with you?" Armstrong asked, determined to find a fault in this man.

"We took the woman from some Cherokees who were returning from Virginia. Because they had failed in their plans to attack the Swanese, they carried off the woman instead. When they were accused of having stolen some horses and saddles and plunder from the back settlers, as they passed through, they blamed the white woman for it," King Haiglar said.

Ignoring Armstrong, he asked the justice, "What will you do with her?"

"No claims have been brought against her that will affect her life. I am informed that she is an indentured servant to a man in Virginia. If that is so, she will not be charged with any offense. I will direct that she be conveyed to her proper owner," the Chief Justice said.

To which King Haiglar replied, "I am glad of it. I am always sorry to lose a woman. The loss of one woman may be the loss of many lives because one woman may be mother to many children."

Some in the audience snickered at his words.

"I have spoken nothing but the truth."

The meeting closed with King Haiglar pledging his continuing support for the commission, and the Chief Justice promising better protection for the Catawba.

In 1762, a small party of Shawnee killed King Haiglar.

Often at night the Catawba men gathered close to the fire while the women and children listened at a distance. Old men told or sang tales of accomplishments to inform and entertain the people.

One old man related this story:

"A party of Seneca Indians, who were our bitter enemies, went to war against the Catawba. In the woods a Catawba warrior stood on a rock. In the distance he could see a Seneca war party coming towards him. When they approached him, he killed seven of them in a running fight. Finally others caught him and began taking him through the woods to their town, triumphant because they had captured the man who had killed their comrades.

"They admired his bravery and treated him kindly on the long trek through the woods, but in the towns they passed through, the women and children were encouraged to whip him severely. He was tried and condemned to die by fire.

"At night he was forced to lie on the cold bare ground with his arms and legs extended in rough stocks. His captors marveled at his stoicism.

"Then one morning when they unpinioned him, he suddenly pushed aside those who stood in his way and dashed down to the water. He plunged in and swam beneath the surface like an otter, rising only when necessary to catch his breath.

"When he reached the opposite shore, he climbed a steep bank with bullets flying all about him. Before he disappeared into the woods, he turned his backside toward them and slapped it joyfully with his hand."

When he said this, the Indians roared with laughter and slapped their thighs.

He continued, "When the warrior returned to where five of his captors were camped, he hid in tall grass and watched until they were sound asleep. He was naked, torn, and hungry, but here was everything he needed--food, clothing, and even weapons. Slowly he crept towards them. Reaching out he grasped a tomahawk lying close to his enemy's back. He grasped it with both hands, raised it above his head, then brought it down, splitting open the Indian's head. Quickly he disposed of the other four.

"After he removed their scalps, he chopped their bodies to pieces. He dressed himself in some of their clothes, then took all of their provisions he could carry.

"Deep in the woods, he rested for several days to recover his strength. Then he ran back through the woods to where he had killed the first seven warriors. He dug the bodies up, scalped them, then burned the remains to ashes.

"Two days later, other pursuing enemies came upon the camp of their dead people. They were shocked to discover the empty graves and burned ashes. In a war council, they concluded that as able as this man was to have killed 12 of them when he was naked and hungry and without a weapon, it was wisest not to pursue him any further, lest he kill them all. They returned home."

Shortly after the beginning of the Tuscarora War, the Saponi, Tutelo, and other Siouan tribes were moved to Virginia. When most of the Cheraw Indians moved in with the Catawbas in 1750, one group refused to join them and continued to live near the north-South Carolina border. It has been speculated that this group is a part of the Robeson County Indians, now called the Lumbees.

By 1784, the once populous Catawba tribe had dwindled to approximately 250.

Chad George-Catawba, SC   Bryan George-Catawba, SC
Young Men's Fancy Dancer   Traditional Dancer
Photos by Ed Sanseverino
1997 Pow-wow

CHICORA-EDISTO

The Chicora were the first recognized inhabitants of what is now South Carolina. The name Chicora apparently came from the Indians themselves, but they are sometimes referred to as Shakori, Chiquola, Chicorana, or Chiquola. They had no written language, but oral traditions were repeated to each generation.

Large numbers of natives gathered on the beach near what is now Pawlely's Island to greet the strange bearded creatures who came ashore. When Gordillo and his men claimed the land in the name of Spain, the Chicoras thought them to be "great sea monsters or gods." After receiving gifts, they befriended the newcomers, but were betrayed when 140 of them were captured to be sold as slaves.

Later the French with Ribaut visited this same place. They invited the Frenchmen to their homes and gave them well-tanned skins, pearls, and baskets made from palm leaves. The French and Spaniards both wanted this land, but eventually they both left.

It was 150 years later that the English came introducing their diseases. Sickness and wars greatly reduced the population of the Chicoras.

The last record of Chicoran activities, was in 1743 at Cherawtown. Chief Eno Jemmy Warrior and his warriors met with the Catawbas. Here the government attempted to force all remaining Indians to move to the Catawba community.

There are gaps in the history of the Chicora tribe as well as many others tribes. This is because those remaining lived quietly, surrounded by the white community. They were aware that they were Indian and knew of their rich history, yet made no effort to be recognized as a tribe.

In the low country of South Carolina, Gene Martin grew up knowing he was neither white nor black--he was Indian. He and other members of his family lived in a stretch of land between blacks and whites. Their written identity was white, but neither the white or the black accepted them.

When Martin decided it was time to announce to the world that he was Indian, others joined him. He had been told all his life by his grandparents of over 200 years of Indianness in his family.

In 1987, largely due to the efforts of Gene Martin, the tribe was reorganized. Gene Martin was elected as Chief. From that time on, Chief Martin has worked for recognition of his tribe. To do this, records had to be kept. Their number has grown from 80 to well over 450. Members live in Horry, Georgetown, Williamsburg, Marion, Clarenden, and Florence counties.

Chief Martin's earnest desire is that his people be recognized and the culture of his people be restored. He has done much to build the Chicoras' pride in their rich heritage.

"Even though there are gaps in their recorded history, the General Assembly of South Carolina has acknowledged the Chicora Tribe as representing the Chicora-Waccamaw Indian Tribes of South Carolina.and has declared April 20 as Chicora Indian Day. Those who can trace their ancestry to 1850, can claim to be Indian.

At the same time, the Pee Dee Indian Tribe was recognized as representing the Pee Dee People.

Edisto

The Edisto Tribe of Dorchester and Collenton Counties of South Carolina readily admits their proper name is not Edisto, but since they live by the Edisto River, they have long been called by that name.

Early Spanish writers and the Grand Council of the Carolina Colony speak of the Edistos as living on Edisto Island. They speak of the Kussos who have lived between the Edisto River and the Ashley River headwaters.

James Miling, in a book titled, "Red Carolinians" refers to "an ancient treaty between the Coosabo Indians and the early settlers of Charles Town."

In 1975, the tribe, in order to reduce the confusion, officially adopted the name Edisto.

Frank Pye
Edisto Vice Chief, SC
Photo by Ed Sanseverino

INDIAN POW-WOWS

When the Indians welcomed the first Europeans to their shores, there was an immediate clash of cultures. The white men failed to recognize their rich civilization and considered them as inferiors.

The Indians had their own religion. Besides various worship ceremonies, for them their religion was their whole way of life. The whites attempted to influence the natives to accept Christianity, sometimes by force. This was difficult for them to understand since the actions of the whites belied their professed doctrine. Strangely enough, some of the natives' religion mimicked the white man's, or did the white man's religion ape the Indians?

The Indians wore fewer clothes, made almost entirely from animal skins. The white man wore more clothes, made from materials such as cotton and wool. They insisted that the Indians cover what they considered the savages' nakedness. When the Indians saw how much easier it was to wear clothing fashioned from ready-made cloth, they no longer wanted to dress the old way.

The Indians taught the white man much about accepting the foods they ate. But the white men also brought exotic foods and introduced the Indians to strong drink.

The white men felt everyone should speak their language, and few learned to be proficient in the tongue of the Indians. This made sense because of the great variety of the Indians' dialects.

Often Indian children were removed from their family

and tribe to attend white schools, but were never seen again.

Largely due to the white man's interference, many tribes became almost non-existent, leaving only a few families clustered together, surrounded by the whites. When the Old Ones repeated the stories of their history, the younger ones weren't interested. In recent years, many of these families joined together, and through oral and written history, organized their tribes and are now recognized by the government.

Over the years, much of their old ways and rich culture was lost. Today, many of the young people no longer speak or even understand their native tongue.

The various tribes have always assembled in councils or conferences for purposes of trading, planning wars, and selecting mates. Today's Pow-Wows, an out-growth of these council meetings, have become one way the Indians have of preserving the old ways and emphasizing their Indianness. It is a celebration of their past with an emphasis on their future. Old friendships are renewed and new ones made.

There is a sort of Pow-Wow circuit, much like preachers used to cover. Pow-Wows are attended by the tribes living in the same general area. Tribes in Maryland, Virginia, North Carolina, and South Carolina, as well as those from as far away as Texas, attend those in this area. Other Indians not affiliated with tribes, those with Indian heritage, and whites are welcome. The Pow-Wows are usually spread out from Memorial Day to Labor Day. Some of those are recognized tribes, while others are clubs or organizations of Indians living in a certain area or attending colleges or universities there.

The session of the pow-wow begins with the parade of dancers. Contestants receive points for participation. The entertainment is held within the arena. It has to be large enough to accommodate the dancers and observers. Before the Pow-Wow begins, the arena is blessed and considered sacred for the duration of the ceremony. Benches are provided for the dancers, who are dressed in dance regalia. Blankets are placed on the benches to mark the reserved spots. No one else is allowed to sit there without an invitation. Sometimes bleachers are provided, or the spectators may bring lawn chairs or sit on blankets on the ground. Children running or playing within the arena is prohibited.

The group is loosely organized with an Arena Director (usually an honored dancer) who helps coordinate the contest events, drum order and dance contests.

The Announcer or Master of Ceremony announces the events, explains the exhibition dances, tells jokes, and performs the usual tasks of the master of ceremonies. It is his duty to keep the ceremony going. There is a time table, but it is not strictly adhered to.

Music is an important part of the Indian heritage. Singing is led by a Head Singer. He must know all the songs to be sung and starts the singing or else appoints someone else to do so. All drummers and singers must wait to join in. Most tribes have a flag song, equivalent to our national anthem. It honors those who have served in the armed forces. Everyone stands while it is being sung. The music starts off with the lead singer, then a second singer, who repeats the lines of the melody on a different or similar key. Dancers keep time to the beat.

According to Gail Lang in the web page, "Native American Indians," some songs are trick songs, fast and slow grass dance songs, shake songs, crow hops, and sneak ups. Some songs are sung with words, but others are "vocables." This began when various tribes couldn't understand each other, yet wanted to join in the singing.

A Head Man and Head Lady Dancer guide and direct the dancers throughout the pow-wow. They begin each dance. Others wait in respect until the Head man and Head Lady begin dancing. Drums are considered sacred to the traditional way of life. Either the old style constructed of hide stretched taut across a frame, then laced with rawhide or the more modern band bass drums are considered appropriate.

There are several basic types of dances. The War Dance was originally restricted to warriors, but today, it is a victory dance, purely social. The Round Dance is a social dance, The dancers move in rhythm in circles clockwise around the drum in a side-step. The faster moving dancers closer to the drum and the slower outside, further away from the drum. They move in rhythm to the drum. In the Rabbit Dance or Two-Step, men and women dance as partners. Couples hold hands, circle the drum, step off with the left foot and drag the right in time to loud-soft drum beats. In the Snake Dance, dancers follow each other in a single line, moving in and out, aping the snake's actions. It tells the story of a snake—a journey through the forest and up the mountains, then coiling up for a rest. It uncoils, then travels on until it comes to a river. Section after section crosses, until even the littlest is across.

Pow-wows are important today because they remind the tribes they are a part of a large group of survivors from the white man's tyranny. The public is welcome. Indian foods are available. Story-telling and information about the tribes are offered. Pow-Wows renew the interest and pride of the Indians in their rich heritage.

OL Durham
Lynchburg, VA
Photo by Ed Sanseverino

Jesse Limon-Larry White Eagle   Darly Fisher Apache VA

Senior Men's Traditional Dancers----- Occaneechi Bank of Saponi Nation
Photos by Ed Sanseverino

Walter Day--Blackfoot--Selma NC

Troy Atkins   Chickhomny Va   Wayne Atkins
Photos by Ed Sanseverino

THE CHEROKEE

Volumes have been written about the Cherokee, the most populous and powerful tribe remaining in the Carolinas. It would be impossible to tell the entire story, so only a few incidents have been chosen to include.

The name Cherokee comes from a Creek word, "Chelokee," meaning "people of a different speech."

Long before the white men made contact with them, the Cherokee built houses, wove cloth, created vessels of clay, and were joined in a tribal confederation. They were organized into the Bird, Paint, Deer, Wolf, Blue, Long Hair, and Wild Potato clans. Their houses were built of reeds and wattle, a circular structure, partially sunk in the ground. In each small tribe were members of each of these clans. Their skin was of copper color, lighter than their other Indian neighbors. They often referred to the Europeans as the "ugly whites."

For them time was measured around the new fire festival. All the fires were put out and the fireplaces cleaned of ashes. Then in an elaborate ceremony, the fires in the village were lighted again to announce the beginning of the new year.

MYTHS AND LEGENDS

The Cherokee's religion, legends, and myths have been handed down for generations. Their religion is their way of life.

The Creation of Mother Earth

In the beginning, the Cherokee were Spirit Creatures living in the Sky Vault which was solid rock. Some creatures had no legs, others were two-legged, or four-legged, or winged.

The creatures reproduced until the time came when it appeared that some would fall off the rock. Beneath it and surrounding it as far as man could see, was a huge mass of water covering the earth, suspended at the four cardinal corners by a cord hanging down from the Sky Vault.

The Great One feared that when the world grew old and the rock was over-crowded, the cords would break and the Rock would fall into the ocean. And all would be water. The Spirit People would die. He told his people, "The cords which hold the earth in place will hold as long as everything is kept in balance, so do not quarrel amongst yourselves or fret yourselves."

But the Great One knew the time was coming when the Sky Vault would be so crowded, it would be necessary to send the Spirit Creatures to live upon the earth. He asked for volunteers to investigate conditions on the water below.

Beaver's grandchild, Water-Beatle, offered to go. He darted here and there in every direction over the surface of the water, but could find no solid ground. Then he dived to the bottom of the water. He came up with mud covering his feet. He shook the mud off. He dived again and again. The mud spread and grew and became muddy islands. Then Water-Beetle returned to the Sky Vault to report to the Great One.

The Spirit Creatures were frightened when they heard Beetle's report. They feared that some would be pushed off the Rock and drown before the mud became dry.

At first the earth was flat and soft and mushy. The animals were anxious to go down below, but the Great One said, "You must wait until the mud becomes solid land."

After more time passed, several Winged Spirit Creatures said, "Let us go see if we can find dry land. We can travel fast and far." They did so, but when they could find no place to land, they returned.

At last the Great One decided enough time had elapsed. He sent out the Great Buzzard, the grandfather of all buzzards. He flew close over the ocean and the muddy islands called earth. When he came to the land where the Cherokee later lived, he was extremely tired and began to flap his wings. As his wings struck the ground, deep holes were made in the mud. These became valleys. Where the mud was piled up became mountains. This is how the great Smokey Mountains were created.

This frightened the Spirit Animals. "What if the whole world becomes mountains?" So they called the Great Buzzard back. The mountains and valleys were there, but other places remained flat.

Now that the earth was dry, the Great Spirit sent down the plants and trees. Then he sent down the Spirit creatures. "You may live here, but you must care for this earth." The Great Spirit gave the creatures the breath of life.

Some creatures chose to remain in the water. They became fishes. Others crawled on the earth. Winged ones became birds. The two and four-legged ones walked upon the earth.

In the beginning there was only one man and one woman, brother and sister. One day the brother struck the woman with a fish, and she brought forth a child. The same thing was repeated for seven days. Then it became obvious that there soon would not be enough room for mankind if this continued. The woman was then allowed to bear a child once each year. Until this time all things spoke the same language and understood one another. But man abused this privilege. As punishment, the Great One made him unable to communicate with the other animals and plants.

Now the plants and animals were all in place, the Great One told them to watch and remain awake for seven nights. The plants and animals tried to do this. Most managed to remain awake through that first night. The next night some dropped off to sleep. At the end of seven nights only the owl and panther and one or two others remained awake. Of the plants, only the cedar, pine, spruce, holly, and laurel were awake to the end.

The Great One gave those animals who had remained awake power to see at night and the plants who had remained awake the ability to retain their leaves during the winter months.

It was still dark, so a sun was hung in the sky above their heads. It was so hot it scorched the Red Crawfish, and the meat inside was unfit to eat. The sun was hung higher, just under the Sky Arch. It was still hot, so the sun was raised higher.

All the plants and trees and creatures, including Man, had their work to do. The Great One was pleased.

But then the seasons changed and the creatures complained that it was turning cold. They desired a fire to keep them warm. The Great One sent down a bolt of lightening which struck a mighty sycamore tree, causing fire to be lodged in its hollow trunk.

But the tree was on an island. "How are we to reach the fire?" they asked. They held a council meeting to decide what they should do. All the animals were present. Those who could fly or swim were eager to go fetch fire.

Raven bragged, "I will bring back fire for all of us." But when he got there and was trying to figure out a way to bring some back, his feathers became scorched. He came squawking back. His feathers remain black to this day.

Screech Owl offered, "I will bring back fire for all of us." He flew high over the sycamore tree. While looking down, his eyes were injured by the heat. He flew back to care for his red eyes. His eyes are still red.

When Horned Owl and Hooting Owl went, they were almost blinded by the fire. No matter how much they rub their eyes, the white rings still remain.

It was decided that none of the birds could bring back fire. Racer Snake offered, "I will bring back fire for all of us." He swam across the water and crawled through the grass to the sycamore tree. He found a hole in the bottom of the tree and went in. The heat and smoke were unbearable, so he went this way and that until he found his way back home.

Then Big Snake Climber offered, "I will bring back fire for all of us." When he put his head in the hole, his head got stuck. The smoke and heat almost roasted him alive, but he wriggled and squirmed until he escaped and went back home. He was so black, after this he was called Blacksnake.

It was so cold, the animals were almost freezing, but no one else offered to go. Then Water Spider said, "I'll go." She had black downy hair and red stripes on her body. She said,

"I can either run on top of the water or dive to the bottom."

The other animals said, "Surely if the birds and snakes could not bring back fire, you cannot."

Water Spider began to weave a bowl from spun thread. She fastened it to her back. She skimmed across the water and through the grass to where the fire was burning. She placed one small coal into her bowl and brought it back across the water to all of the animals. To this day, she had retained her basket.

The Great One was pleased. He was proud of His creation and of His creatures.

Mark Day sitting on Jadculla Rock   Photo by Robert Day

The Slant-Eyed Giant- -Jadculla Rock

The slant-eyed giant's name is Judaculla or Tsulkalu. He is over twice as tall as any man. He is married to a Cherokee woman and has two children. He owns all the game animals in the Great Smokey Mountains and is a great hunter. When he is thirsty, he drinks the creek dry. This accounts for dry beds where water used to flow. When he is hungry, he is capable of leaping from one mountain-top to another in search of game. He lives with his family in a cave where he farms and watches over his domain from the top of Tanasee Bald.

At one time, from his mountain-top, Jadaculla saw hunters coming into the valley of Caney Fork Creek. His angry roar because these midgets were invading his land could be heard for miles around.

He sprang down determined to destroy the intruders. As he landed in the valley, he reached out with such force to steady himself that he left his hand print in the soft soapstone rock.His hand print and other strange markings, called petroglyphs, can still be seen there today. The rock is protected from the elements by a simple shelter, but it is easily seen about four miles east of Chllowhee in Jackson County, North Carolina.

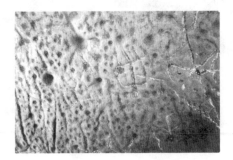

Jadculla Rock   Photo by Robert Day

YUNWI ISUSDI : LITTLE PEOPLE

Some question the existence of the Little People. But although many Indians do not speak of them to strangers, to most of the Cherokee, the Little People are quite real. They are short--barely reaching to a man's knee, handsome with long hair and well-formed bodies. They are usually white but can be Indian or black.

They live in caves or under piles of rocks or behind a waterfall.

In the beginning when the plants and animals left the Sky Rock to live upon the earth, there was only one tobacco plant. All the people came to this place to obtain their tobacco.

Then the Little People stole the plant and carried it to Chimney Rock on the South Side of Hickory Nut Gorge in Rutherford County, North Carolina.

Tobacco was an important part of their culture, so a young man offered to go fetch the plant. The Little People killed him on the spot and left his body in the hot sun to rot.

A Cherokee conjurer turned himself into a humming bird and went to find the tobacco plant. He found the bones of the dead young man and restored him to life. Then the conjurer and the young man brought back huge quantities of tobacco to the Cherokee land where it flourishes to this day.

There are basically three kinds of Little People: the Laurel People, the Rock People, and the Dogwood People.

The Laurel People are generally mischievous. They tickle and pinch children in their sleep causing them to giggle. They can be heard outside the house or in the woods playing, making music, dancing, and laughing. They are happy and want everyone else to share their happiness. They sometimes tease people by leading them astray.

The Rock People are angry because others have invaded their space and have stolen wood from them. To get even they steal children and throw rocks at people or their possessions, but their aim is poor.

The Dogwood People bring a lesson for us all. If you do good for someone, you must do it out of a willing heart, not for personal gain. These are the ones who watch over the aged and the children.

They don't like it when people disturb them at their homes. If a person finds out where they live, the Little People will throw a spell on him, and he will be dazed from that time on.

Some say that if you actually see one of the Little People, either you or someone dear to you will die within a week.

Sometimes at night, you may hear the Little People happily chatting as they bring in your corn or do other tasks for you. But you must not go out to investigate, because if you do and see them, you will surely die.

Old people often leave out food for the Little People to eat. In return, the Little People will help them by washing their dishes or sweeping the floors. Sometimes they are seen out of the corner of one's eye. When old persons die, it said the Little People take them by the hand to lead them over.

What is their purpose in being here? They are here to teach us how to live in harmony with nature and with others.

The Uktena Monster

The Uktena giant serpent is so dangerous that even to look at it could make the looker die of fear. It has a scale-covered body as thick as a tree trunk. A pair of antlers are on its head. A huge crystal clear jewel (the Uluhsati) with a red center is in the middle of its forehead.

To possess the Uluhsati insures the owner great success in his hunting, in his love life, and other factors of his life. Often it enables the owner to predict whether someone will live or die.

It has one draw-back, the bright light from the Uluhsati has such power that it will befuddle a person's senses so that he will run towards it and become its victim.

Many men have attempted to kill the Uktena and steal its jewel, but only one man has succeeded.

A Shawnee conjurer, who was a Cherokee prisoner, was promised his freedom if he would find the Uluhsati and bring it back.

He searched until he finally located it asleep on a mountainside in Georgia. He built a circular trench around it and set fire to pine cones around it. Then he shot an arrow into its body.

After the body had rotted and the creatures had devoured the carcass, leaving only the magic crystal, he took the crystal back to the Cherokee.

No white man may ever lay eyes on this jewel.

NANCY WARD, CHEROKEE CHIEFTAINESS

Nantegi was the niece of Attakullakulla (Little Carpenter). When her people, the Cherokee, were at war with the Creeks, her hatred of the enemy was so strong that, in spite of being ordered to remain hidden, she followed her husband Kingfisher into battle.

She made herself useful. She chewed her husband's bullets, knowing this would cause great, tearing wounds in the enemies' bodies. To her dismay, in the midst of battle, her husband was struck down. Instead of cradling his head in her arms until he ceased breathing, she grabbed his gun and ran shrieking towards the enemy. Her aim was true. Creek after Creek fell dead from her bullets.

When the Creek warriors saw this, many fled in terror. She was invincible. None of their bullets struck her. "She is crazy," one Creek said.

Another said, "Spirit Warriors make her shots ring true and protect her from harm."

The Cherokee fighters praised the young woman who had fought so well. At the next tribal council, it was decided that young Naynehi should be made Ghighau (Beloved Woman), an honor ordinarily bestowed on an elderly woman for her years and wisdom. In those days, 45 was considered old.

The Ghighau was seated next to the Council fire with the authority to speak at Council and even to decide the fate of captives. By raising the swan's wing [the emblem of her authority], she could pass judgment or overrule decisions made by the Council. It was a heavy responsibility. Alone at night, sometimes she wondered if the gods who spoke through her were always right.

In a treaty, the whites promised to leave the hunting lands to the Cherokees. Nanyehi shook her head in disbelief. "The whites no keep their promise," she said. "Old way of life for Indian become a thing of past." She was right.

As the whites deliberately slaughtered the elk and buffalo, they took more and more of the Indians' hunting land.

Naneyhi surprised everyone by marrying a white trader, Bryant Ward. "Why you marry that man?" the chief asked.

"We must learn to live the white man's way." She adopted the name of Nancy Ward. She soon realized that marrying Ward was a bad decision. He was no young and handsome like her warrior husband had been. As time passed she could barely remember what her first husband's face looked like, but she remembered his shining hair worn loose and waist-length with a single braid in front of his left ear, the sign of the warrior.

When the chief and other leaders showed their disapproval of her marriage, Nancy had an answer for them. "I will live my own life my own way," she said.

"Ward saw a good thing in the young Indian widow," the chief said. "It was the only way he could remain on Indian land."

A daughter Elizabeth was born to this union, but the chief and other leaders were right, within a few years the marriage ended.

Nancy had learned much from her new husband. The whites numbered as the trees on the mountains, but the Cherokees were few. Fighting the whites would be useless. They would not just disappear as the creeks had, they were there to stay.

At Council, she said, "Fighting them only destroys us.

They are many, we few. Only way to live at peace is to become as they are. Raise crops and cattle. Prepare and eat white man's food. Then they will accept us without war."

At Watauga River at Sycamore Shoals, Daniel Boone, through a half-breed interpreter, spoke to more than 1,000 Cherokees.

He and his men spread out six wagon-loads of trade goods on blankets. "For land beyond the mountains, we give you many gifts," Boone said.

The young warriors coveted the woolen goods, glass beads, rifles, and cases of whiskey set before them. They discussed it among themselves. "If he want that far-off land, give it to him. Foolish man. No can buy land. No can own land. If he want to trade for something we no own and he cannot own, why not?"

It has been said that a chief took Boone aside and said, "We have sold you much fine land, but you have much trouble if you try to live there."

So the agreement was signed.

In 1776 when the whites were at war with England, the British approached the Cherokees. "We are your friends. Join with us to fight the intruders."

Their plan was to use the Cherokees, 500 Creeks and 500 Chickasaws to attack the frontiers of Virginia and North Carolina. This could have changed the outcome of the war.

Although many no longer listened to her advice, Nancy Ward warned the white residents of Tennessee River Valley to flee to the forts for protection. A white woman and her boy were captured. The boy was horribly burned at the stake. Mrs. Bean was bound for the same fate. But Nancy Ward rescued the lady before she could be killed.

From that time on, the young warriors despised Nancy

Ward.

She was wise beyond her time. She insisted, "Soon Cherokee will have to leave this land, move further west as have so many of our cousins."

In 1785 at a Council at Hopewell, South Carolina, the Cherokee made the first of several treaties with the U.S. government. In it they gave up claim to all land then occupied by settlers. A new boundary was defined and the government promised to restrain its citizens from further trespass.

Nancy Ward, at the request of Old Tassel, spoke. "I have a pipe and a little tobacco to give to the commissioners to smoke in friendship. I have see much trouble in the late war. I am now old, but hope yet to bear children who will grow up and people our Nation and have no more disturbance. The talk I give you is from myself."

There was no halting the great flood of settlers coming to occupy the land of the Cherokee.

TREATIES

For nearly 100 years after De Soto's visit in South Carolina, the Cherokees had little contact with the white man. A small party of Spaniards traveling through the Cherokee country listed no permanent settlements.

The English settlers when they moved in, feared and hated them, harming the Indians whenever they could.

As more and more settlers came, they required more and more land, pushing the Cherokees off.

The ink was barely dry on one treaty before another one was drawn up. By 1835, the Cherokees had been forced to sign treaties giving up vast areas of land that included parts of West Virginia, Virginia, Kentucky, Tennessee, North

Carolina, South Carolina, Georgia, and Alabama.

In 1752, A.G. Spangenberg, a Moravian Bishop, searched out the Piedmont region of North Carolina for settlement. He wrote that the land between the Catawba and Yadkin Rivers was much frequented by the Catawbas and Cherokees for hunting. He said these Indians were quite different than those in Pennsylvania. "There no one fears the Indian, unless he is drunk. Here the whites must needs fear them. If they come to a house with only the wife at home, they are insolent, and the settler's wife must do whatever they bid. Sometimes they must come in such large companies that a man who meets them is in real danger."

The Moravian records of July 1755, tell of an incident which happened during one of their evening services.

Mr. Banner, who had been out for several days looking for strayed horses, arrived late to the meeting. After eating, he left to go home. Then about 4 o'clock the next morning, the Brethern were awakened by Mr. Banner, frantically crying, "They're gone. My wife and children, they're gone!"

"What do you mean, they're gone?" his brother asked, tucking in his shirt tail.

"When I arrived home, my wife and children weren't there. And someone had taken everything he could carry from the house. I searched the near-by woods, but I couldn't find them. I didn't know what else to do, so I came here."

"You did the right thing," Brother Loesch said.

The Brethern gathered around the poor man and comforted him as best they could. "Since we are all up anyhow, before we organize a search party, we'll have our morning worship," Brother Loesch said.

They knelt in prayer, beseeching their heavenly Father for His care and protection. The Bible text for the day suited the situation. At the close of the service, Brother Loesch ordered the gun fired twice and the blowing of the trumpets. This was the first time the trumpets had been used since they had been brought down from Pennsylvania.

"Now if anyone within hearing is still asleep, they will hear the trumpets and come to help," Brother Loesch said.

As the trumpets began blowing again, they heard someone calling. They ran towards the sound. Imagine their joy when they found Mrs. Banner and her four children. She staggered under the weight of a child on her back. Another was in the arms of an older child.

Neither Mr. nor Mrs. Banner could speak for weeping.

After Mrs. Banner and her children had eaten and rested a bit, she told her story. "During the night while I was waiting for my husband, the dogs began barking and running back and forth from the house to the woods. At first I locked the door, fearing it was Indians. But then I thought maybe someone was injured and went forth to investigate. Stones flew past me, barely missing my head. I ran back into the house and grabbed up the children and ran out the back way for the woods. I saw three persons enter the house, but I couldn't see if they were Indian or white. I didn't wait to find out."

"How did you find this place?" her husband asked, knowing she had never been there before.

"I knew it was situated in this direction, so I found the path and followed it through the woods."

After the morning worship and breakfast, Mr. Banner, accompanied by Brother Loesch and Lischer, went to the Banner house to see if it was safe for his family to return, and to warn his neighbors.

The Banner house, which was along the Virginia trail

was plundered 14 times during the French and Indian War.

In 1760 some settlers spied a party of six or eight Cherokee warriors near Salisbury. They watched as the Indians entered a deserted house. They surrounded the house and posted themselves behind a fodder stack and outbuildings so they could see the door and the chimney top. When they were all situated, those closest to the house, threw burning torches upon the roof.

The dry shingles caught fire and soon was blazing furiously.

The Indians had to choose if they wanted to die by bullets or by fire. One of them called out to his companions, "it is better that one should die that the rest may live. I will go first. When it is safe, follow me."

He pushed the door open and rushed out, dodging and running in a zigzag course. The settlers emptied their guns firing at him. He fell dead, blood oozing from his many wounds.

While the settlers were reloading their guns, the other Indians ran to safety.

The Moravians' first settlement was near the present day Winston-Salem. Three miles west of there, they began a second settlement called Bethania. 1760 was a year of fierce Indian fighting.

Several miles up the Yadkin River, William Fish, his son, and a man named Thompson were riding through a canebreak on a trail. They were on their way to the Fishs' farm to collect at safe places along the Yadkin. Suddenly a party of Indians ambushed them. Fish and his son were both killed. Thompson turned his horse around and made his way down the Yadkin. Indians were in front of him, at his right side and his left side. He leaned low, hugging his horse's mane, he spurred his horse and dashed to the river. He crossed over and climbed out on the other side. There he plunged into the woods, but he soon got lost.

At last he reached familiar surroundings and made his way to Bethabara where men gathered around him and helped him off his horse. He slumped to the ground, exhausted from his experience and from loss of blood.

"Indians down the Yadkin. They killed Fish and his son. The woods are filled with them. I escaped through the river."

He had been struck by two arrows, one in the hip and the other in his back between his shoulders. Thompson was cared for by Dr. Bonn, who removed the arrows and treated his wounds. But infection set in, and he died.

It cost him his life, but his giving the alarm saved the lives of many settlers.

The next day 50 persons came to Bethabara for protection. When a military company went out to bury William Fish and his son, they came across a large party of Indians. So instead of the burial, they visited several families who had refused to leave their farms. When they heard about the Fishes, they changed their minds and accompanied the soldiers to the blockhouse and safety.

In the morning two men--Lashley and Robison--left the blockhouse to feed their cattle. They were killed by Indians.

Lashley's 13-year-old daughter went to her father's house to milk the cows. She was frightened by nine Indians. They saw her as soon as she saw them and chased her. In the woods, she took a sudden turn where she temporarily escaped them. But the Indians back-tracked until they found her trail through the wet grass. She made her way up and down the branches of the river in her neighborhood with them after her. She found Town Creek Ford and plunged into the creek. She followed it until she came to a steep bank where cane hung heavy over the side, creating a sort of cave for a hiding place.

She could run no further. Gasping for breath, she decided to remain where she was. The Indians followed her trail to the water, where they lost it.

When it got dark, the Indians gave up the pursuit, and she was able to come out of her hiding place and begin to search for the blockhouse. When she finally found it, she proceeded with caution, lest she be mistaken for the enemy.

The guard saw her and was about to fire, when she yelled, "Don't shoot! It's me, Lashley's daughter. Is my father here?"

When the guard saw who it was, he helped her inside to safety.

Women gathered around her. They had feared her dead. "Honey, are you all right? We were so worried."

"My father?" she was almost afraid to ask.

"Your father is dead. The Indians killed him." She had expected to hear this, but still it was tragic news.

Near the mouth of Smith's River in Rockingham County, the Indians killed two men on Bean's Island Creek. The Indians were close to them. They could see that the white men had forgotten to reload their guns. They rushed at them and killed another before they could reload their guns. Hicks shut himself up in his house to protect his wife and child.

The Indians broke open the door. The man fought valiantly, but he was killed. The Indians then took his wife and two-year-old boy prisoner. With other Indians as captives, they were taken to Indian towns on the Tennessee. One of the braves who had admired Hick's bravery in trying to defend his family, took the little boy in his arms and said, "His father was a brave man. I will see that his son is kept safe." He carried the child on his back to his Cherokee town. Later General Waddell rescued this woman and child and returned them to their people.

A Company of 50 Rangers were employed by the state to travel over the country to protect the settlers. They rode horses, carried rifles and muskets, and wore hunting shirts and buckskin leggings.

One day a ranger named Hampton and several other rangers came across a man who was lying a little off the path. "What's your name?" Hampton asked. He could see that the man was injured.

"William McAfee. I left the fort with another man to hunt in the Hollows. We were attacked by some Indians. I was shot. I can't move. I think my thigh is broken."

"Where's your horse? We'll help you on it and take you to town."

"He ran off. I've been lying here for hours, waiting for help."

One of the rangers searched the area and found the horse dead of his wounds.

"It's 33 miles from the fort or any place of safety, but we'll help you." They lifted him on one of their horses and took him to the fort. His wound was tended to and he lived for many years, although he limped the rest of his life.

A similar thing happened to a 16-year-old boy named John Williams. He was hired to keep camp and cook for two men named Linville while they went hunting. Indians came upon them and killed the Linvilles. Williams was shot in the thigh. He knew he was hurt, but he didn't realize that the bone was broken.

He ran off. After about 50 yards, the bone snapped, and he fell. Luckily the Indians did not go in search for him. Instead they gathered up their skins and guns and went off, taking the best of the horses.

Williams crawled on his belly back to camp, dragging his injured leg behind him. There he found an old horse the Indians had not wanted to bother with. Williams managed to grab hold of a piece of rope dangling from the horse's neck. Carrying it in his mouth, he painfully edged over to a log. Here, gritting his teeth to keep from screaming, he managed to climb on the horse.

He rode for five days in that condition, eating nothing but a few blackberries. Finally he found a house. He was exhausted, weary from loss of blood and pain. After his wound was almost healed, another Indian alarm came, and his leg was broken again. Eventually his bone healed, and he lived to an old age.

The Brown family were traveling through Cherokee country to reach a tract of land that had been issued to the father as an award for fighting the British in the battle of the Guilford Courthouse.

The family traveled in two big boats; the father, mother, two brothers, three sisters, and five other white men. They were met by four canoes bearing Creek and Cherokee Indians.

Since the Indians didn't appear to be carrying weapons and showed a flag of friendship, the father wasn't afraid. A man, who was part-Indian and part-white, spoke, "Do not fear, we come in friendship and will do you no harm."

So the Indians were allowed aboard the Browns' boats. Suddenly the Browns were surrounded by weapon-carrying Indians. An Indian came after Joseph and his father. He cut off the father's head and took Joseph prisoner. Joseph's mother and sisters and young brother were carried off in one direction and he in another.

An old white man named Turnbridge met Joseph and his captors on the shore. He argued, "Do not destroy the boy. He will make a good servant. Let me take him home with me."

The old man's wife, a French lady who had grown up with the Cherokee, welcomed Joseph to her house.

Soon a group of drunken warriors appeared at the door demanding the prisoner. "We wish to have a frolic," they said.

Joseph shook with fear. He understood little of what they were saying, but he surmised they meant him harm. "This boy is my son's prisoner. You cannot have him," Turnbridge said.

Turnbridge's son was a tall warrior with many scalps to his credit. The old man's wife cried out. "Do not despoil my house. If you must kill him, take him away some place else." She appeared more concerned about her clean house than Joseph's life.

They agreed to take him about four miles off to a place called Running Water for their frolic. When they got there, Joseph fell to his knees. "Please spare me my life. I'll be your servant for the rest of my life." The Indians, deep in conversation, ignored him.

Then Joseph saw one of the Indians smile at him, and this gave him hope that he would not be killed.

At nightfall the Cherokee chief returned and was angry at what had taken place. "I, myself, have never stained my sword with white man's blood, only the Shawnee. Besides it

184

would be foolish to kill a white boy so near this village. The whites would kill us all and burn our town."

Turnbridge's warrior son had arrived. "I take the boy as my prisoner."

The chief decided, "The boy must remain here as an Indian. I will be responsible for him. He will call me Uncle and Tom Burnbridge, Brother. His hair must be cut, and he must dress like an Indian."

Joseph eagerly agreed.

The old French woman shaved his head except for a scalp lock, then bored holes in his ears. She gave him a length of cloth to wind about him as a breech-clot.

A fat old woman waddled in and warned, "You will rue the day you brought that wolf pup into your home. When he is grown he will return with his kind and destroy us all."

Joseph labored in the fields, never complaining, lest the Indians change their minds about allowing him to live.

Soon word came to the whites that young Brown was living at a Cherokee village as a slave. They set about to bargain for his release. His freedom was purchased, and he was reunited with his mother, sisters, and brother who were also released. His littlest sister had become so fond of her surrogate mother that she had to be torn from her arms to be given to her natural mother.

Later, as the fat old squaw had predicted, Joseph Brown guided the white army to destroy their town.

THE REMOVAL

The state of Georgia was particularly abusive to the Cherokee. There are two possible reasons for this. One was the idea that there was gold hidden in the wilds of Cherokee country. The other, probably more important reason, was the need of the whites for the land held by the Indians.

Andrew Jackson aided the forces in Georgia who finally pushed the Indians off their lands. Strangely enough, Jackson's life had once been saved by a Cherokee by the name of Chief Junaluska at the Battle of Horse Shoe Bend. Junaluska had taken 500 Cherokee scouts and helped Jackson win the battle, leaving 33 of them dead on the field. During the battle, Junaluska had driven his tomahawk through the skull of a Creek warrior who had Jackson at his mercy.

In payment, in September of 1776 the militia destroyed more than 36 Cherokee villages, leaving no one alive.

Later in an attempt to prevent the transfer of the tribe to Oklahoma, Chief John Ross sent Junaluska as a representative to speak to President Jackson asking for protection for his people. Jackson agreed to see him, but his manner was not friendly. He allowed Junaluska to give his plea, then he said, "Sir, your audience is ended. There is nothing I can do for you." So Junaluska left in disappointment.

Back home, a sickly widow woman with three small children was told she must go with the soldiers. She gathered her children at her feet and prayed for them. Then she patted the family dog on the head. With a baby strapped on her back and leading a child with each hand, she began the long walk to the blockade.

It was too much for her to bear. Her heart gave out, and she sank to the ground with the baby on her back, still holding the others by the hand.

When Chief Junaluska (who had saved Jackson's life) saw what had happened, tears gushed down his cheeks, and he lifted his face toward heaven. "Oh, my God," he said, "if I had known at the Battle of Horse Shoe what I know now,

American history would have been written differently."

The Cherokee's cause was championed by Henry Clay, Daniel Webster, and Davy Crockett. But they failed. On May 10, 1838, General Winfield Scott ordered the removal of all the North Carolina Cherokees except the Oconaluftee, who were considered citizens of the state instead of the Cherokee nation. The remainder were to be rounded up and placed in stockades until they could all be brought together to be moved west. In the stockades, the Indians were fed poorly prepared food of a kind they were not accustomed to. Many died.

Those who were still alive, were ordered to leave. This was the beginning of the "trail where we died." It was heart-breaking, the future uncertain. Some put up a fight. There are several versions of what happened to an old man called Tsali.

In the general round-up, Tsali and his wife and sons were ordered captured. Along the trail to the blockade, a soldier prodded the wife along with a bayonet.

"Hurry up, old woman," he said as he jabbed her. Tsali knew it was useless to argue with the soldiers. He quietly went among the other prisoners, saying, "We must escape before we get to the blockade. When I make the signal, will you join me in a revolt?"

Since he spoke Cherokee, the soldiers didn't catch on to his plan. The attack was sudden. Each warrior attacked the soldier next to him and attempted to wrest his gun from him. One or two soldiers were killed by Tsali's two older sons, Nantayalee Jake and Nantayalee George. The soldiers ran. The Indians escaped to the mountains.

General Scott made a bargain with Euchella of the Oconaluftee. As agreed, he and his warriors soon found the cave where Tsali and his family were hidden with others of his clan.

Euchella reported back to General Scott, "The cave entrance is guarded."

So Scott contacted Colonel William Thomas, known to be a friend of the Cherokees. "They are your friends. Tell them that if they will surrender Tsali and his sons for punishment, the remainder will be allowed to stay where they are until the government comes to a decision. Otherwise, I will send 7,000 troops in to flush them out."

When Thomas considered the alternative, he decided to talk to Tasli. One story says that Thomas strode past the guards at the mouth of the cave. He was respected, so no one bothered him. He sat down on a rock beside Tasli.

"Unless you surrender yourself and your sons, the soldiers will hunt you and your clan down like rats in a barrel and kill you all."

In order to save his people, Tsali surrendered. General Scott ordered him and his two oldest sons killed. He forced Euchela's men to shoot them, "so they will know we mean business."

A version of this story is told each season at Cherokee in an outdoor drama, "Unto These Hills."

At various times, hundreds of Indians from other blockades also escaped to the mountains. Those who didn't die of starvation, subsisted on roots and berries.

Nearly 17,000 Indians were assembled in the various stockades awaiting removal to the west. The removal began in June of 1838. Between 10 and 25 per cent died of disease, hunger, and hardships on the trail west. The last party left December 4, 1838. Those who could fled to the mountains where they joined those already there. More than 1,000 remained behind.

Anton Anderssen, a Cherokee instructor at Oakland

Community College of Warren, Michigan, said in the USA Today, "Our Native American people were rounded up like cattle into cramped prisons, beaten, starved, whipped, raped, sodomized, and tortured. Soldiers rejoiced in their victory over us by holding a parade where they flaunted mutilated Indians' sexual organs. We were run out of our lands and forced to march across the country on foot in the dead of winter to Indian reservations, where we were starved and deliberately given disease-soaked blankets."

Murder had been committed. In fact, 4,000 murders had been committed, making this a blot on American history which can never be erased.

For a long time after the removal, those who were left behind struggled to exist. They lived in caves or huts. Since they were not considered as US citizens, they couldn't legally hold title to their lands, so they put their land titles in the hands of friends they could trust. One of these was Colonel William Thomas.

Thomas' father had been drowned before Thomas was born, so he grew up homeless. When he was 12 years old, he contracted to tend a trading post owned by Felix Walker. He was promised keep and $100 for three years service. However, at the end of the contract, Walker didn't have the money to pay him, so he was given several law books as partial payment. These books changed young Thomas' life.

Yonaguska, who was a chief of the Cherokees, noticed the young boy and took him into his home and adopted him. From him, Thomas learned not only the language but also the ways of the Indian.

Later he set himself up in business at Qualia where he became friend and counselor to the Indians and continued to study law.

This made him a valuable asset to the Cherokee. He devoted his life to their cause. He allowed the Cherokees to live on the land he held in trust for them and to develop it. For a time, he became a Cherokee chief. Later he became a United states Senator and was able to get a law passed making them citizens.

Colonel Thomas had large tracts of Indian land in his name by this time, but he also had large personal debts.

After he died, Thomas' creditors attempted to take the Indians' land to pay his debts.

A delegation of Cherokee men to Washington to plead for their land. The government gave them title to their land and added more tracts to it.

The Cherokee Reservation is known as Qualla Reservation. The Cherokee pay taxes on this land and develop it as any other citizens, but they cannot sell it except to another Cherokee.

Today, approximately 8,000 of the eastern Band of the Cherokee live on Qualla Boundary, next to the Great Smokey Mountain National Park. It is a well-known tourist spot, offering the Occunaluftee Indian village, a museum, an outdoor drama, and a casino. The children have their choice between Indian schools or the regular government schools.

The Eastern Band is recognized by the Federal Government.

Chief Henry, a full-bloodied Cherokee, is said to be the most photographed Indian in the world. He has been available for photos for 51 years. His picture has appeared in the National Geographic and other nationally known magazines. Chief Henry readily agrees that the Cherokee did not use wigwams or wear feathered headdresses, but he goes along with what the tourists expect.

Cherokee winter hut. reconstructed behind the museum at Cherokee by the use of old-time tools.   Photo by Mark Day

HARRAH CASINO   Photo by Mark Day

THE LUMBEE

When the first white settlers reached the piney woods of southeastern North Carolina along the Drowning Creek [Lumbee River], they were surprised to find Indians who spoke English, lived in log cabins, dressed like whites, and attended Baptist and Methodist Churches. They tilled small fields of poor land which surrounded their towns.

Who were these people who lived like whites yet appeared to be Indians?

Mr. Hamilton McMillan, a Robeson County lawyer, was the first to put forth the theory that these Indians were descended from Sir Walter Raleigh's Lost Colony. When John White returned to England for much-needed supplies and more colonists, he left behind approximately 100 colonists. When he returned several years later, he found the place deserted with no trace of the missing settlers. Although numerous attempts were made to locate them, 400 years later, no one actually knows their fate. McMillan suggested they had joined with the Indians and moved to Robeson County, retaining their language.

Because of white man's diseases, the Hatteras, Machapungo, and Coree tribes had become so small, many had joined other tribes and moved south. Here they, with escaped Negro and Indian slaves, joined those Indians already living in the area. Because he believed they came from the whites and the Croatan Indians, McMillan called them "Croatan." He said, "They held their land in common. They occupied the country as far west as the Pee Dee, but their principal seat was on the Lumber, extending along that river for 20 miles."

The Lumbee Tribe, on their web page states, "The ancestors of the Lumbee were mainly Cheraw and related Siouan-speaking Indians who lived in the area of what is now Robeson County since the 18th century."

The Lumbee are the most populous of the six North Carolina recognized tribes.

In 1754 at Drowning Creek, 50 families lived on land they had no titles to. They were a lawless people, who eked out a living by farming poor land, surrounded by swamps.

Then one day, a surveyor entered the area. He was met by angry men. "Who are you and what are you doing here?" the leader asked.

"I'm a surveyor come to view vacant lands."

"As you can easily see, these land are not vacant, they are occupied."

The surveyor puffed with authority. "They belong to the government which hired me to survey them."

At this, one of the Indians, pulled a gun from under his coat. The surveyor ran, his coat-tails flapping in the wind. He was fast, but not fast enough to outrun the Indian's speeding bullets.

He was struck and fell down dead.

A circular distributed a short time later, made no reference of Indians as the culprits, but called them "mixed-bloods."

In about 1735, white settlers began moving in the area. Tradition says that the tribe took part in the Tuscarora War with Colonel Barnwell and brought back several Mattamuskeet prisoners who were absorbed into the tribe. They took part in both the Revolutionary and 1812 Wars.

In 1835, the state of North Carolina passed a new constitution which prohibited "persons of color" from voting, serving on juries, testifying in court against whites, bearing arms, or even learning to read and write. The constitution did not specifically mention the Lumbee, but it was understood to include them. Because they were considered second class citizens, others could easily take advantage of them.

Since they were not white, they were excluded from serving in the army during the Civil War, but they were used as a labor force. After a yellow fever epidemic killed many blacks, the planters objected to the loss of their expensive slaves, and the authorities drafted the Lumbee to build the forts along the Lower Cape Fear River.

Many of the Lumbee hid in the swamps to avoid doing forced labor. They were joined by escaped Union soldiers. Gradually the group became pro-Union.

Because the Lumbee could not come out of the swamps to farm, their families suffered. In 1864, a 16-year-old Lumbee, Henry Berry Lowry and two of his brothers stole some hogs from a wealthy farmer. They carried them home, slaughtered, and barbecued them. Escaped Union soldiers were among those who attended the feast.

The next day, the farmer who owned the hogs came to the Lowry farm, searching for evidence of his missing livestock. Near the barbecue pit, he discovered what he was looking for--hog ears with his mark upon them.

The farmer approached the Lowry brothers, waving the ears before him. "See--I told you so. You stole my hogs. Here is the proof."

In answer to his accusation, the Lowry brothers drew their guns. The farmer dropped the hogs' ears and ran.

He did not press charges of theft. But the next day, he reappeared, accompanied by a conscription official to draft the men into labor camps.

Henry Lowry and his brothers, warned of their coming, hid in bushes. When the conscription official and the farmer got close enough, the Lowrys fired by ambush and killed them both.

Now they were wanted for murder. They hid deeper in the swamps. Their small band included Lumbees, blacks, and at least one white--his wife's 14-year old brother. If Henry Lowry was married to a white woman, this further angered the officials. From this time on, the Lowrys declared war on the Confederacy. They hid out in the swamps and came out only to rob and steal, much as Osceola in Florida.

They assaulted the Robeson County Courthouse in Lumberton and seized guns and ammunition and raided other prosperous plantations, but avoided the small farms. They shared their meager provisions with poor blacks, whites, and Indians--regular Robin Hoods.

They fought the Home Guard and the Ku Klux Klan. The North Carlina Home Guard militia came to the Lowry farm to capture Henry Berry Lowry and his band. Since the outlaws were hiding in the swamps, they failed to find the Lowrys. However, they did find proof of theft, the gold head of a cane stolen from a wealthy planter. The entire household was arrested and taken to a nearby plantation to be tried.

The Home Guard voted to execute Henry Berry Lowry's father and one of his brothers. They were taken into the woods and killed. This further infuriated Henry and his remaining family.

Since at that time, General William T. Sherman was advancing towards them, the other prisoners were released.

To the Lumbees, the coming of the Union Army was looked forward to with great anticipation. They believed that Sherman would recognize their accomplishments and reward them. But Sherman's army did not differentiate between friend or foe. They took food and livestock belonging to rebel planters and loyal Lumbee alike.

So when the army moved north, the Lumbees were in even more desperate shape than before. The Lowry band continued to steal in order to feed themselves and their families. Other destitute men joined with them.

Everyone expected that the end of the war would grant pardons to the Lowry band. Instead, former Confederates, who were still in power, relentlessly pursued the Lumbee outlaws. Since the Lumbees were Republicans, they expected the government would punish the Home Guard for their unfair treatment of them. The Lumbee were disappointed when this didn't happen.

The government decided that the Lowry band were common criminals who stole for their own good. Henry Berry Lowry and his band returned to the swamps for years of exile and violence.

Henry Berry Lowry became a well-known hero. It was claimed he stole from the rich to give to the poor, made daring attacks to jails to release members of his band, then disappeared into the swamps.

In July, the militia rounded up some of the Lowry women to hold as hostages. Eighteen members of the militia paused to rest at Wire grass Landing in Robeson County. A lone canoe came down the river towards them. It was Henry Berry Lowry. The militia opened fire. Lowry jumped into the water on the far side of the canoe and using it as a shield, swam toward the militia, all the while firing his gun over the side of the boat.

Eventually the militia withdrew with their wounded. Henry Lowry later secured the release of the Lowry women by threatening to capture white women to replace them.

Lowry's last raid took place in February of 1872 when he robbed a store in Lumberton. Here he took food as he usually did, but he also took a safe containing $22,000.

The next year, many of the gang were killed or captured, but Henry Berry Lowry was never seen again. Did he die from wounds or illness? Did he quietly live out his life on the family farm? Or did he live in the swamps on the money he had stolen? No one will ever know for certain.

Henry Berry Lowry is considered a folk hero. He gave to the Lumbee people a sense of pride in themselves. He unified their feeling of being a separate race of people.

Since the Lumbees were considered as mulattos, they were forbidden to attend the white schools. The parents refused to allow their children to attend the Negro schools, so for the most part, the children grew up unschooled.

In 1885, Mr. Hamilton McMillian worked on the Legislature to pass official recognition for the tribe. In 1896, the South Carolina Legislature recognized them as Croatan. This did much to improve the quality of life among the Lumbee. They were ambitious and many became wealthy. But until 1947, they were denied access to white restaurants, bath rooms, or water fountains. Some establishments such as train depots, were required to have three water fountains--one for whites, one for Negroes, and one for Indians. This required six rest rooms.

In 1953, North Carolina changed the tribe's name to Lumbee. Although they probably came from mixed ancestry, today the Lumbees are justifiably proud of their race and of what they have accomplished.

There are over 40,000 members, the largest tribe in North Carolina, east of the Mississippi, and ninth largest in the nation. They live in Robeson, Hoke, and Scotland Counties in North Carolina, but many have moved to other places where they are employed in a variety of occupations.

Reggie Brewer   Lumbee   Talina Locklear

Photos by Ed Sanseverino

OCCANEECHI BAND OF SAPONI NATION

Over 1,000 years ago, an ancient people called Yesah migrated from the Ohio River valley to the east, then settled the Piedmont areas of what is now Virginia and North Carolina. On islands in the Roanoke River [near Clarksville, Virginia], they formed the villages of Saponi, Totero, and Occaneechi. Large timber was available. The soil was rich, and their livestock flourished on a kind of pea which remained green all winter.

The middle island was the Occaneechi. The natives living there were called by this name. The village was strategically placed, located in a position to control all trade from the east to the west and west to the east. The Occaneechi were a war-like tribe. Their influence, language, and religion spread far and wide.

In 1670, John Lederer paused there, but afraid for his life, escaped during the night.

In 1673, Virginia trader Abraham Wood sent James Needham and Gabriel Arthur to open trade with the Indians in the West country. They arrived at the island home of the Occaneechi, who refused to allow the Virginia Indians to pass through. So Needham and Arthur left, accompanied by only one Appomattox Indian.

Arthur remained at the Tomahitan town, while Needham returned to Virginia.

On Needham's second trip, he angered one of his guides, an Occaneechi Indian called Indian John. John killed Needham.

Later, Arthur passed by with the Tomahitan chief and 18 others of that tribe, laden with furs. When they reached the scene of Needham's death, they found his possessions scattered about on the ground. As they attempted to gather them up, they were surprised by four Occaneechi. Arthur and his party ran and hid in some bushes until it was safe to leave.

In May of 1676, Nathaniel Bacon led a rebellion against the colonial government of Virginia. He was jealous of the trade of furs and copper between the Governor of Virginia and the Occaneechi. He led his militia into the land of the Occaneechi to destroy their trade monopoly.

The Occaneechi moved south and settled along the Eno River [near Hillsboro, North Carolina]. John Lawson visited them there in 1701. Here the Occaneechi remained for several decades.

In 1713, Virginia signed a treaty of peace with the Occaneechi, so they returned to Virginia. Governor Spotswood attempted to convert the Saponi tribes to Christianity.

The tribe made several trips back and forth between North Carolina and Virginia and lost their title to their Virginia reservation.

By the middle 1700s, the tribe settled on the line of the North Carolina-Virginia border [Greenville, Brunswick, Mecklenburg, Granville, and North Hampton Counties]. Here many of the tribesmen received title to their ancestral lands.

By the 1780s to escape discrimination, the Occaneechi left Virginia, traveling down the Old Trading Path to their former lands on the Eno River, where they had once lived [Alamance and Orange Counties].

Eventually this area became known as the "Texas" community. The Saponi people were formally reorganized in 1984 as the Eno-Occaneechi Indian Association, Inc. In February of 1995, the name was formally changed to the

Occaneechii Band of the Saponi Nation, a more accurate reflection of their ancestry.

At Hillsboro, archaeological excavations, begun in 1983, has revealed the old village which once stood there. This was supported by grants from the National Geographic Society and the Summer School and the College of Arts and Sciences at the University of North Carolina at Chapel Hill.

The tribe is now reconstructing the village one-half mile from its original site, so as not to disturb the ground. The reconstruction is an exact replica of the old village, down to the last pole. This is the only known such project being carried out by direct descendants of the original tribe.

Mr. Lawrence A. Dunmore III is Tribal Chairman, and Mr. John Blackfeather Jeffries is Vice-Chairman. The tribe is ruled by a 13 member board of elders. They are at the present time endeavoring to become the seventh recognized Indian tribe of North Carolina.`

Their Pow-wows are among the largest in this area.

Assistant Chief John Blackfeather Jeffries Occaneechi-Saponi, Hillsboro NC
Photo by Ed Sanseverino

202

GRAND ENTRY POW-WOW OCCANEECHI BAND OF SAPONI
HILLSBORO NC 1997
Photo by Ed Sanseverino

Annette Jeffries
Occaneechi-Saponi
Photos by Ed Sanseverino

Assistant Chief John Jeffries Blackfeather
Sarah Stryker, Sabrina Stryker AsheboroNC

HALIWA-SAPONI

The Haliwa-Saponi or Halifax-Saponi Tribe is descended from the Saponi, Tuscarora, and Nansemond People. They live in the Halifax and Warren counties of North Carolina. The majority live in the Meadows community which was first established in the late 1700s.

Educating their young was a problem since they were neither white nor black. In 1882, the Bethlehem Indian School, the only one of its kind at that time in North Carolina not on a reservation, was established, supported by the state.

They have been recognized as a tribe since 1965. Retaining their Indian culture is paramount among their efforts. To do this, they have one of the largest Indian Pow-Wows in the state.

They have programs to serve the elderly, children, and those needing job training and withdrawal from alcohol or drugs.

They are one of North Carolina's six recognized tribes.

Rev Clark Stewart Chickhomny VA   Photo by Ed Sanseverino

CARTERET COUNTY INDIANS

Carteret County on coastal North Carolina has no Indian Pow Wows, but its people have long been interested in the Indians of this region. Information concerning its earliest inhabitants comes from tradition, but mostly from the Indian digs and artifacts found there.

Since 1987, the North Carolina State Historic Preservation Office has reviewed or been involved in 15 archaeological studies in the county. Approximately 700 prehistoric features such as houses, burials, and cooking pits have been verified.

It is obvious from the large mounds of shells and artifacts found that Indians either lived there year around or seasonally.

The Coree blood still flows among many of those living in Carteret County. Some families who cannot trace their genealogy back to the Coree, retain the high cheek bones of their ancestors. For many years it was considered disgraceful to be part-Indian, so it is difficult, if not impossible to trace where the Indian blood entered their families.

On Cedar Island, tradition says that the first George Styron had children by an Indian lass he kept as his wife. Another story is that when the Indians were chased from the island, they left a baby girl behind. One of the Styron families took her in and raised her. When she was grown, a Styron man married her. Since John Styron lived on the Banks while Indians still occupied the area, it is believed his wife Abigail was probably Indian.

Then there is the story of two Day families who lived on the Southeast end of the island. They had no sons. One day an Indian man who had an infected leg wound, remained there with the wives while the men went to Hog Island for a hunting-fishing trip. Nine months later, both Day women gave birth to dark-complected sons.

Times have changed somewhat, so that today many acknowledge and are proud of their mixed heritage.

Bogue Field

Shelly Point Site, located on the Marine Corps Auxiliary Land Field at Bogue, Carteret County was originally recorded by Littleton and Mattson in 1969. The concern of the continuing impact of military activities and shoreline erosion caused the US Army Corps of Engineers to cause an investigation. They were to establish boundaries, identify cultural affiliation, document deposits, and assess its potential as a historic site.

Lithic and ceramic materials indicated the presence of Early, Middle, and Late Woodland, possibly even earlier occupancy.

Evidence of at least three prehistoric structures were found.

Across the county line in Onslow County, the Uniflite Site was discovered by Tucker Littleton in 1963. Research shows that the site had been occupied in late spring and early summer where large quantities of shellfish were consumed.

The Coree Remnant

When Sir Walter Raleigh's First Expedition arrived at North Carolina's Outer Banks in 1585, they were met by the Hatteras and Coree Indians. The Corees occupied the territory from Cedar Island to Harkers Island on the mainland and from

Cape Hatteras to Cape Lookout on the Banks, including most of what is now Carteret County. Governor Archdale in 1686 described the Corees as a "bloody, barbarous people."

When the explorers returned to England, they took two native Americans with them; Manteo of the Hatteras tribe and Wanchese, a Coree from Harkers Island.

Jerry Lee "Turtle" Faircloth, Sr. of Atlantic, North Carolina claims the Coree tribe still exists, that the Corees were not offered a treaty or given a reservation as were all other tribes.

He has appeared before a Congressional committee asking for recognition and a reservation for his people. He has also written letters to the President and to the Governor, but he has received no encouragement from his quest.

He says that when he was a child on Harkers Island, Mrs. Merry Ann Willis told him, "Old Man Harker and his sons killed the last three full-blooded Coree men on Harkers Island and buried them in a single grave."

Even after the last three Harkers Island men were killed, Indian women and part-Indian children still existed there as well as scattered about the county.

In his booklet, *Silent Warriors, the Coree Indians,* Chief Faircloth tells us much about the way the Coree Indians lived, their dwellings, the food they ate, they way they hunted, and their religion. He says he has a collection of pipes found in a shell mound or along the shore. According to him, the ceremonial pipes were blessed by the Medicine Man or Woman, whichever one they had at that time. Ceremonial smoking took place in either a meeting house or ceremonial lodge, usually to celebrate a marriage or burial.

According to Chief Faircloth, they smoked a mixture of tobacco, grapevine, willow, and marijuana leaves, depending upon the ceremony. He says that smoking marijuana and mushrooms mixed with the regular tobacco sometimes enabled the men to see into the future. The ceremonial pipes were molded from clay, then baked to harden.

Since the days of the Hunters and Gatherers, Indians had come from inland to Harkers Island and other coastal areas to gather shell fish. After they feasted on the oyster and clam meat, they used the shells as dishes, weapons, and tools. Piles of these discarded shells were used to form two bridges on Harkers Island. The bridge at Shell Point stretched over two miles to almost reach the shores of Core Banks. Construction was halted when the white man came and changed their way of life.

The other bridge was at the western end of the island at a place called Rush Point. It framed an enclosed area known as Pearl's Creek and was used as an oyster and clam bed and a shelter for water fowl. Hundreds of arrow and spear points found there attest to the fact that it was a great fowl hideout.

Truck loads of shells from Harkers Island were used to form five miles of road bed on the island. Loads were transferred by scow to Hyde County to be used on roads or burned and ground up to be used as fertilizer.

Marshallberg

In 1985, as a part of the 400th Anniversary of the first attempted English settlement in North America, John and Esther Valentine of Marshalberg [near Harkers Island] displayed a collection of Indian artifacts throughout the county.

Mrs. Valentine said, "Sometimes I would take a bucket with a shovel and plastic bags when I walked along the shore.

Especially after a storm, I found things the waves had washed ashore. Once I found some bones and broken pottery lying on the sand."

"What did you do with them?"

"I carefully lifted the specimens, not touching them, and placed them in a plastic bag. At home I put the bag in a shoe box and sent it to the Smithsonian. I never dig for artifacts," she said. "I just collect items lying on the sand."

"What did the Smithsonian say?"

She showed me their reply: "The bones are indeed human and appear to be those of an adolescent. The associated pottery is a little hard to date but probably is grit (sand) tempered, fabric impressed ware datable from the Middle Woodland Period or about AD 500-1000 (or slightly earlier)."

"Then what did you do with the bones?" I asked, wondering if I could see them, or if they were a part of the display at the library.

She was shocked that I had asked. "I buried them, of course. I took the shoe box and its contents and buried it where I found it. My father was a Christian and taught us to respect life. When we were children, we were told never to touch any bones we found at the Indian mound."

Douglas L. Rights is his book, "Americans Indians in North Carolina," speaks about a shell mound on Harkers Island, marking the feasting place of Indians in former days. He says that clam and oyster shells predominate, with frequent occurrence of conch shells and the bones of fish and turtles. The well-defined layers are often marked by fire pots, pebbles, and animal bones. Intermingled with the shells were stone tools, arrowheads and several Indian skeletons.

Burned at the Stake

According to a story told to Hellen Russell Garner by her father, Briant Russell, a young white boy died as the result of being burned at the stake [Russell's Creek outside of Beaufort].

Two Russell boys left home before sunrise one morning in or about the year of 1714 to go hunting in the woods near the shore of the Newport River. They came to a small clearing in the woods. The older boy ordered his brother, "You stay here. I'm going deeper into the woods. Maybe I can pick up the trail of a deer."

He was following an animal trail some distance away when he heard a frightful scream. It was his brother! He was in trouble.

Remembering what his father had taught him, instead of crashing panic-stricken through the thick woods, warning the enemy of his presence, he carefully and quietly loaded his gun, and slowly crept in the direction of his brother's screams.

The younger boy's screams were terrifying. The birds were strangely silent. The older boy hoped the silence wouldn't warn the enemy--whatever it was--of his presence.

He crept closer. What he saw would leave a lasting impression on his young mind, causing nightmares for the remainder of his life.

In a small clearing his eleven-year-old brother was tied to a stunted pine tree, his arms bound behind him. Dry brush was piled loosely about his feet, lit and smoldering but not yet burning rapidly. Four Indian braves gleefully danced about, enjoying the young boy's agony.

The older boy took careful aim. This would be his only

chance. As the flames reached his brother's pants legs, he squeezed the trigger.

The Indian he had aimed at yelled and fell, grabbing his leg. The boy alternately screamed and shouted, making as much noise as he could, hoping to confuse the Indians into believing there were many white men coming from all directions to rescue his brother.

The braves were young and confused by the racket. They dragged their wounded comrade into the dense woods where they disappeared. The older boy dropped his gun and raced towards his brother. He ripped off his coat to beat at the flames. Then he smothered the remainder. His brother had fainted. With his hunting knife, the older boy cut the rawhide which bound his brother's bleeding wrists to the tree.

As his brother fell, he dragged him away from the scene. His hands got burned when he touched his brother, but he didn't even notice it until much later.

His brother was burned so severely that his skin fell off where he was touched. But he was still alive. The older boy picked up his gun and shot three times to summon help. Had he done all he could? Maybe he shouldn't have left his brother alone in the clearing. It was ridiculous but somehow he felt responsible.

He heard someone come crashing through the woods. It was his father. The older man's eyes widened with shock when he saw his son. With tears in his eyes, he put his coat around the boy, lifted him in his arms, and carried him home.

The younger child later died as a result of severe burns and shock.

Indian Beach

In October of 1968, on Bogue Banks outside Salter Path, when Earl and Wayne Thompson were having a drainage ditch dug near the eastern end of Paradise Bay Mobile Home Park, red sand appeared instead of the white, yellow, or gray sand usually found.

As boys are wont to do, Earl Thompson's son began playing in the sand. He soon found spearheads and arrowheads. But when other artifacts, including four complete skeletons, numerous teeth, arrowheads, tomahawks, a shaving stone, and a peace pipe were found, the authorities were informed.

Word of the burial mound leaked out, so sheriff's deputies and Marine Corps MP's were called to guard the area.

In November Dr. Jeffrey Coe led an archeology team which came to the area to investigate.

They found several more skeletons as well as other artifacts. One skeleton was found with the bony fingers of one hand grasping a conch shell, and the other a tomahawk.

The mound was said to be between 500 and 800 years old.

South River

One of the largest private collections of Indian artifacts has been assembled by the Carraway family of South River. These objects were found around the South River, Garbacon Creek, and Brown Creek areas. The Carroways don't dig for artifacts, just gather them, often after a storm.

This area was once plantation or farm land. Many

Indians artifacts, plowed up in the past, were carelessly discarded. It is evident that many Indians either lived in this area or else gathered there for trading and to feast on oysters.

Indian skeletons and parts of skeletons have been found. Archeologists from Chapel Hill and Greenville worked the site for some time. Some graves only held one body but others contained several skeletons. An arrowhead was found lodged in a skull of one body and another in a rib cage.

No complete pieces of pottery have been found, but pieces of shard of at least five different textured designs are in the collection. They are cord-marked, fabric-marked, and linear-checked pieces. The color varies from light tan, brown, orange, red, and black.

Mrs. Dollie Carroway in her book, *South River, A Local History From Turnigain Bay to Adams Creek* explains that the Indians held a ceremony called "Busk" each year. At this time, houses were cleaned, and old clothes and pots were discarded. This may account for the significant amount of shard pottery found. Some of the pottery has been dated to about 600 AD.

Pipes and portions of pipes are often found. Some are inscribed and one even shows teeth imprints. The pipes were made from red clay found in this area and color varies as does the pottery. Traders pipes were made from a mold, but have not survived time as the clay ones have. They were made with long stems to keep the heat from the bowls away from the face. If it was smoked by several different people, each person bit off a piece of the stem to make it sanitary for the next person. These pieces weren't discarded but used as beads.

Beads of clay, shell and stone have been found in that area.

Arrowheads and spearheads have been are of stone, quartz, and flint. Many of these are quite aged and of different kinds. All implements made of stone had to have come from other places, since no stones were found in this area. Stone clubs, axes, and mauls are also in the collection.

Pestles, grinding stones, and nutting stones have been found which were used to prepare food.

Stone drills, scrapers, hoes, spades, celts, discoidals, sinkers, gorgets, and arrow shaft straighteners are also in the collection. Even two stones which were used as moccasin lasts to shape moccasins as they were being made were also found.

Mr. and Mrs. Carraway and their two sons have displayed their exhibits and discussed early Indian life in this area to school classes and other groups who are interested.

Turnagain Bay

Between Cedar Island and South River is a body of water with the interesting name of "Turnagain Bay." There are two stories as to the origin of its name.

Since the early 1700s, white people have been living at South River. During the Tuscarora War, there was one old farmer who owned several hogs. One morning one of his young pigs was missing. He was disturbed. Could a wild animal have come out of the woods and taken his pig?

The next morning another of his pigs was gone. This was serious business. He needed his hogs to feed his family. So he decided to catch the thief, whatever it was.

That night, he hid in a ditch near his hog pasture, armed with his shot gun. It was a long, miserable night. As the sky to the east lightened with streaks of yellow, pink, and orange, he saw a figure slinking from the woods, towards his sleeping pigs.

As it drew near, he saw it was a young Indian man. The intruder grabbed a squealing young pig, and carrying it under one arm, he raced towards the woods. The farmer stood up and shouted at the Indian, "Stop, or I'll shoot!"

For his answer, the Indian stopped, turned again, and lifting his breech clot, "mooned" the farmer. The farmer raised his gun and shot. The Indian streaked for the woods, still carrying the pig. So this is one explanation as to how Turnagain Bay received its name.

The second story comes from Cedar Island's unofficial mayor, Ronald Goodwin. He says that many years ago, Indians lived in the field in back of where his house now stands. This was during the time when Indians and settlers lived side by side in comparative peace, probably about the time of the Tuscarora War, but possibly even later.

Since the field where the Indians lived look fertile, the settlers decided they wanted this land for themselves and chased the Indians out. The Indians took their women and children and moved to Indian Ditch, still on Cedar Island.

But still the whites were not satisfied. More settlers came. They needed more land, so they chased the Indians further away to what is now called Turnagain Bay.

It was here that the Indians decided they had been pushed far enough; it was time to make a stand. So they turned again and fought, determined to hold their land.

But after a fierce battle, the Indians were defeated and retreated to Croatan. This is why Turnagain Bay was given its name; it's where the Indians decided to turn again and fight.

The Witch

A story told by Mrs. Janet Daniels of Cedar Island concerns a lady named Amassa Styron Daniels.

Shortly before the Revolutionary War, a baby girl was found washed ashore on the sound side of the island. Apparently the child had been placed on a wooden bread tray with a few of her clothes by someone on a boat, hoping the child would be found.

She appeared to be Indian. A family by the name of Styron took her into their home and raised her as their own.

But the girl was never like other children. Not only did she appear different, she acted strange. She had what people called the "sixth sense." She knew things she couldn't know because they hadn't happened yet. This frightened the other children, who ran home and told their parents, who told their neighbors, who told ...... Soon everyone on the island was aware of the girl's oddity.

They became convinced she was a witch. She had the ability to cause all sorts of harm to those who displeased her. One day when she went to a neighbor's house to get a pail of milk, nobody was home. She became angry and placed a hex on the cow. When the lady of the house went out to milk her cow that evening, the cow was dry.

Another time she was invited to dine with a family. Someone said something which displeased her. She glared at the plates of food on the table. Until then, the food was perfectly good, but now it was spoiled.

She had the ability to cause people to become ill by giving them the "evil eye."

This lady really existed. She became the second wife of Randall Daniels. He had been married before and had several children by his first wife. Amassa and Randall had no children together. She appears in the 1850 census as head of household, so her husband had died by that time.

All during her life, from the time she was a young child, she occasionally became afflicted with a curious ailment. The only cure that worked was an old Indian remedy mentioned by John Lawson. A hole was dug and water allowed to seep in. When it was deep enough, she was immersed in the water, covering her head. When she was removed from the water, she was well.

When she was 79 years old, while home alone, she was stricken with such an attack. Since no one was there to dig a hole for her and lower her into the seeping water, she died.

THE LITTLE SMITHSONIAN

Martha Fay Goodwin Day of Cedar Island has a small building devoted entirely to artifacts she has collected over the years. Many of these are of Indian origin gathered along the shore. The pipes are of various shapes. An expert says the red clay pipe in the first picture was made before Christ was born. The spear head in the same picture is made from metal, probably acquired from the whites. She has arrowheads, clay marbles, broken pottery and an old Indian jug, beautifully shaped, complete but cracked. There is a variety of tools, including the cores of conch shells shown in the basket picture.

The following photos were taken by Phillip Day.

AUTHOR'S NOTE--WHOSE LAND IS IT?
(From *A WALK IN THE NIGHT*)

Daniel, our number three son, was special in many ways. He seemed to think more deeply and care more deeply about things than most people did. He never blindly accepted what was told him as truth. He had his own ideas about almost everything, and I never knew exactly where these ideas came from.

No matter where we lived, we tried to return to Cedar Island every year or so, just to walk along the shore on the end of the island where we used to live, eat a picnic lunch, and go home refreshed.

Sometimes we visited some of the older relatives and talked about the "old days" on Cedar Island long ago, even before we lived there.

On one such day, I walked along the shore towards Lewis' Creek. Since the tide was high there wasn't much room to walk along the shore, so I returned to where I had started. I sat down comfortably on a water-washed juniper log, my bare heels digging into the soft wet sand, gazing out across the rumpled sea green waters of the sound, thinking about nothing in particular, just enjoying the peace and serenity of the moment.

My sons had walked down the beach in the opposite direction. Dan returned and sat on a protruding hunk of cement, perhaps a front door step from a house, long ago devoured by the tide.

"Dan," I said, "can you imagine what it was like here before the white man came? Can't you almost see the Indians in a canoe going across the sound to the Outer Banks to go fishing or hunting?"

Dan didn't reply immediately. He stood up, picked up a broken clam shell and heaved it far out into the water. Then he said, "We don't belong here."

"What do you mean? This end of Cedar Island is a part of the Wildlife now, so we have as much right here as anyone else does. In a sense, it belongs to us."

"It belongs to the Indians."

"Why? That was a long time ago."

"What difference does it make when it was? If something was stolen, it was stolen whether it was today or 400 years ago."

"But, Dan, you know it was necessary. The white people had to have a place to live. Besides the Indians weren't farming and building houses and really using the land."

"How do you know? I think they were. I think they raised corn and vegetables much like the white people did. I think they had permanent houses here, not so very different from the first white people. And even if they didn't, they were living here. It was their land."

"Why was it their land? Were they always here? Didn't they come from some place else and take it away from the animals?"

"Animals don't count, we're talking about human beings."

"You talk like I was the one who did it. My ancestors didn't even live here, yours did. So if anyone was responsible, you were."

Dan faced me and accused, "You said yourself that Indians once lived in Iowa. You even mentioned finding arrowheads there when you were a child."

"Well, I guess so. But it wasn't you or me, it was our great-great-great-great-great grandparents, so why are we responsible?"

"We just are. And what's more, we weren't satisfied with stealing their land, we made many of them slaves and killed others."

"That went both ways. Think of all the white people the Indians scalped."

"And who started that? It was the white people. They started the whole thing. In most places the Indians welcomed the white men into their homes and treated them as brothers. Then the white men came and killed some and chased the rest away."

"But, Dan, that's just the way life is. Nations, like people, come for awhile, then they are gone. Look at history."

"I **am** looking at history. At the history of the white man's cruelty to the Indians."

"Okay, Dan, supposing what you say is right, what can we do about it now?"

"Give it back to the Indians."

"That's ridiculous."

"Well, it just isn't right."

"Dan, I've always heard that your Dad is part Indian, so you are too. Maybe that's why you like nature so much, hunting and camping out, and just being in the woods and on the water."

"Could be. I like people too. But sometimes when life gets too complicated, I just like to get off by myself and enjoy nature. To watch animals in their natural habitat, trees which seem so solid and permanent and watch the sun which rises and sets without anyone interfering or having to wind it or set it, just to rough it for a day or so away from all my problems and irritations."

"I guess you are part-Indian. So, Dan, if you're part-

Indian, you do belong here. This land belongs to you."

We sat in silence, pondering what we had discussed.

Then Dan, staring off towards the distant horizon, mused, "The Indians were right. No man can own land. For thousands of years, it was occupied only by animals. Then came the Indians. And now the white man. I wonder who or what will come next."

BIBLIOGRAPHY

Alderman Pat, Nancy Ward: Cherokee Chieftainess, Overmountain Press, Johnson City TN, 1978.

Anderssen Anton, USA Today, 9/4/97.

Angie Debo, A History of the Indians of the United States, U of Oklahoma Press, 1970.

Candal Patrica Ed, The Reclamation of a Native Tribe, Gail Lang Do It With Pride http://www.pride net.com/

Carraway Dollie C, South River-Local History from Turnagain Bay to AdamsCreek, M&L Designs, Alpha Graphics, Fayetteville NC.

Clark Walter, State Records of NC 1776-1790 Raleigh NC 1895-1905.

Deacon Richard, The Discovery of America.

Ehle John, Trail of Tears, Anchor Books, Doubleday 1988.

Explorations, Descriptions, and Attempted Settlements of Carolina 1584-1590, StateDepartment of Archives and History, Raleigh NC 1953.

Faircloth Chief JL "Turtle" Sr, Silent Warriors, The Coree Indians, Atlantic NC.

Garriett JT & Michael, Medicine of the Cherokee, Bear & Co Publisher, Santa Fe NM 1996.

Gragg Rod, Planters, Ppirates, & Patriots, Rutledge Hill Press, Nashville TN 1985.

Katz William Loren, Black Indians, Aladdin Paperbacks, 1986.

Lawson John, A New Voyage to Carolina, notes by Hugh Talmange Lefler, U of NC Raleigh NC 1967.

Lee E Lawrence, Indian Wars in NC, The NC Charter Tercentenary Comm. Raleigh NC 1963.

Lewis Taylor & Young Joanne, The Hidden Treasure of Bath Town, Taylor Lewis & Associates, 1978.

Morrison Samuel Eliot, The European Discovery of America, Oxford University Press, 1971.

National Geographic Vol 173, No 3 Exploring our Forgotton Country, pg 330, March 1988.

Oberlin Steve, Madoc Welsh Prince, sdo@iquest.net 1996.

Perdue Theda, Native Carolinians, The Indians of NC, NC Div of Archives & History, NC Dept of Cultural Rescources, 1985.

Rights Douglas, The American Indian in NC, John F Blair Publisher, Winston-Salem NC 1957.

Rossman Douglas A, Where Legends Live, Cherokee Press, 1988.

Siler Margaret R, Cherokee Indian Lore & Smokey Mountain Stories, Teresita Press, 1993.

Stephens Kay Holt Roberts, Judgement Land: The Story of Salter Path Book II, Bogue Sound Books, Swansboro NC 1989.

Stick David, The Outer Banks of NC 1584-1958, The U of NC Press, Chapel Hill, NC 1958.

South Stanley A, Indians in NC, NC Dept of Cultural Resources, Raleigh NC 1980.

Underwood Tom B, The Story of the Cherokee People, Cherokee Publications, 1961.

Warner Jayne, A Consideration: Was America discovered in 11... by Prince Madoc AB Owain Gwyneth of Wales, History 2a for Dr. Spear 9/21/95.

Walser Richard, NC Legends, NC Dept of Cultural Resources, Div of Archives & History, 1980.